# The Green Witch Herbal

Your Complete Guide to Discovering Wiccan Herbal Magic and how to use Herbs in Contemporary Witchcraft.

## AMY HARMONY

© **Copyright 2019 - All rights reserved.**

The content contained within this book may not be reproduced, duplicated or transmitted without direct written permission from the author or the publisher.

Under no circumstances will any blame or legal responsibility be held against the publisher, or author, for any damages, reparation, or monetary loss due to the information contained within this book, either directly or indirectly.

Legal Notice:

This book is copyright protected. It is only for personal use. You cannot amend, distribute, sell, use, quote or paraphrase any part, or the content within this book, without the consent of the author or publisher.

Disclaimer Notice:

Please note the information contained within this document is for educational and entertainment purposes only. All effort has been executed to present accurate, up to date, reliable, complete information. No warranties of any kind are declared or implied. Readers acknowledge that the author is not engaging in the rendering of legal, financial, medical or professional advice. The content within this book has been derived from various sources. Please consult a licensed professional before attempting any techniques outlined in this book.

By reading this document, the reader agrees that under no circumstances is the author responsible for any losses, direct or indirect, that are incurred as a result of the use of information contained within this document, including, but not limited to, errors, omissions, or inaccuracies.

The cover has been designed using **Freepik.com** resources.

To my grandmother,
who taught me to seek magic
in the little things.

# CONTENTS

Introduction ........................................................................1
Chapter I  A Brief History of Wicca................................3
   The Father of Wicca ........................................................4
   The Main Beliefs and Traditions of Modern Wicca .7
Chapter II The Power of Herbal Magic ........................11
   What is Herbal Magic? ...................................................12
   What is an Herb? ............................................................13
   The Five Elements in Herbal Magic............................14
   Astrology and Herbs.......................................................15
   The Magic of the Moon .................................................19
Chapter III  Working with Herbs ....................................23
   WORKING WITH HERBS .........................................24
   A WITCH'S GARDEN ................................................25
   The Makings of a Witch's Garden...............................25
      Add a Garden Altar ...................................................26
   Themes for a Witch's Garden.......................................31
      An Elemental Garden ...............................................31
      A Moon Garden.........................................................35
      Astrological Garden...................................................37
   A Witch's Garden For All Spaces and Situations ....38
      Utilizing a Large Space for a Witch's Garden......40
      Privacy.........................................................................41
      Wrap-around Garden ...............................................42
      Creating a Small Witch's Garden ...........................42
      A Patio or Balcony Garden .....................................43

A Small Courtyard Garden ........................................ 44

Indoor Garden ........................................................ 45

HARVESTING, DRYING, AND STORING HERBS ................................................................... 47

Harvesting ................................................................ 47

Once-Off Harvesting: .............................................. 48

Bulk Harvesting ....................................................... 48

Drying ...................................................................... 49

Slow Drying Method ............................................... 49

Fast Drying Method ................................................ 50

Storing ..................................................................... 51

A WICCAN'S TOOLS ............................................. 52

1. An Athame ......................................................... 52

2. A Cauldron ......................................................... 52

3. A Staff or A Wand .............................................. 53

4. A Robe ................................................................ 53

5. Candles and Crystals ........................................... 54

6. A Pentacle ........................................................... 54

7. A Book of Shadows ............................................ 55

Chapter IV A List of Magical Herbs ........................... 57

HERBS LISTED BY NAME .................................... 58

Alfalfa (Medicago sativa): ........................................ 58

Angelica (Angelica archangelica L.): ....................... 58

Ash (Fraxinus): ........................................................ 58

Astragalus (Astragalus propinquus): ....................... 58

Adam and Eve Root (Aplectrum hyemale): .......... 58

African violet (Saintpaulia): .................................... 59

Allspice (Pimenta dioica): ....................................... 59

Adder's tongue (Ophioglossum): .........................59
Aloe (Aloe vera): .........................................59
Ague Root (Trichanthera): ..............................59
Almond (Prunus dulcis): ................................59
Alyssum (Lobularia maritima): .........................59
Amber (Amber): ..........................................59
Apple and Apple Blossoms (Malus domestica): ..60
Avocado (Persea americana): ...........................60
Basil (Ocimum basilicum): ..............................60
Bay Leaf (Laurus nobilis): ...............................60
Birch Bark (Betula): ......................................60
Bay (Laurus nobilis): .....................................61
Blue Sage (Salvia azurea): ...............................61
Cardamom (Elettaria cardamomum): ................61
Chamomile (Matricaria chamomilla): ................61
Chives (Allium schoenoprasum): ......................61
Cinnamon (Cinnamomum verum): ...................61
Cloves (Syzygium aromaticum): .......................62
Cedar (Cedrus): ...........................................62
Cherry and Cherry Blossom (Prunus avium): .....62
Club moss (Lycopodiopsida): ..........................62
Comfrey (Symphytum): .................................62
Coriander (Coriandrum sativum): .....................62
Cumin (Cuminum cyminum): .........................62
Caraway (Carum carvi): ..................................62
Cayenne (Capsicum frutescens): .......................63
Daisy (Bellis perennis): ...................................63

Dandelion (Taraxacum): ............................................63

Dill (Anethum graveolens): ......................................63

Daffodil (Narcissus): ................................................63

Elder (Sambucus): ....................................................64

Elm (Ulmus): ...........................................................64

Eucalyptus (Eucalyptus globulus): ..........................64

Fern (Leptosporangiate fern): .................................65

Fennel (Foeniculum vulgare): .................................65

Figwort (Scrophularia): ...........................................65

Foxglove (Digitalis): ................................................65

Frankincense (Boswellia sacra): ..............................65

Frangipani (Plumeria): ............................................65

Garlic (Allium sativum): ..........................................66

Ginger (Zingiber officinale): ...................................66

Hazel (Corylus): .......................................................66

Holly (Ilex): .............................................................66

Hyssop (Hyssopus officinalis): ................................67

Hibiscus (Hibiscus rosa-sinensis): ...........................67

Honeysuckle (Lonicera periclymenum): ...............67

Ivy (Hedera): ...........................................................67

Irish moss (Chondrus crispus): ...............................67

Jasmine (Jasminum): ...............................................68

Knotweed (Fallopia japonica): ................................68

Lemon (Citrus Limon): ..........................................68

Lavender (Lavandula): ............................................68

Lilac (Syringa vulgaris): ..........................................68

Lily (Lilium): ...........................................................69

Lime (Citrus aurantifolia): ............................................. 69
Leek (Allium porrum): .................................................. 69
Luminous Moss (Schistostega pennata) ............... 69
Mint (Mentha): ............................................................. 69
Mandrake (Mandragora Officinarum): ................. 69
Mistletoe (Viscum album): ....................................... 70
Meadowsweet (Filipendula ulmaria): ..................... 70
Moonwort (Botrychium lunaria): .......................... 70
Mugwort (Artemisia vulgaris): ............................... 70
Nutmeg (Myristica fragrans): ................................. 71
Nettle (Urtica dioica): .............................................. 71
Orange and Orange Blossom (Citrus): ................. 71
Orchid (Orchidaceae): ............................................. 72
Oak (Quercus): ........................................................... 72
Parsley (Petroselinum crispum): ............................ 72
Peppermint (Mentha balsamea): ............................ 72
Pennyroyal (Mentha pulegium): ............................ 72
Pansy (Viola tricolor subsp. hortensis): ................ 73
Poppy (Papaver somniferum): ................................ 73
Patchouli (Pogostemon cablin): ............................. 73
Primrose (Primula vulgaris): ................................... 73
Rose (Rosaceae): ........................................................ 73
Rosemary (Rosmarinus officinalis): ....................... 73
Ragwort (Jacobaea vulgaris): ................................. 74
Rue (Primula vulgaris): ............................................ 74
Sage (Salvia officinalis): ........................................... 74
Saffron (Crocus sativus): .......................................... 74

Sweet pea (Lathyrus odoratus): ................................ 74
Spiderwort (Tradescantia): ....................................... 75
Spanish moss (Tillandsia usneoides): ..................... 75
Spearmint (Mentha spicata): ................................... 75
Star Anise (Illicium verum): .................................... 75
Thyme (Thymus vulgaris): ...................................... 75
Tuberose (Polianthes tuberosa): ............................. 75
Vanilla (Vanilla planifolia): ...................................... 76
Violet (Viola): ............................................................ 76
Vervain (Verbena): ................................................... 76
Valerian (Valeriana officinalis): ............................... 76
Vetivert (Chrysopogon zizanioides): ...................... 76
Witch Hazel (Hamamelis): ..................................... 77
Wormwood (Artemisia absinthium): ..................... 77
White Sage (Salvia apiana): .................................... 77
Willow (Salix): ......................................................... 77
Wintergreen (Gaultheria procumbens): ................ 77
Wood Aloe (Aloidendron barberae): ..................... 78
Yarrow (Achillea millefolium): ............................... 78
Toxic Herbs .................................................................. 78
Dangerous Herbs for Pets .......................................... 79
Dangerous Herbs for Pregnant Woman: ................. 80
Chapter V How to Use Herbs ....................................... 83
WICCAN USES FOR HERBS ................................ 84
Magical Oils ................................................................. 85
Hot Oil Method ...................................................... 85
Cold Oil Method ..................................................... 86

Safety Tips For Magical Oils ...................................87

  Using Magical Oils ....................................................88

 Incense and Smudging .................................................90

 Charms, Sachets, and Dream Pillows ........................93

  Dream Pillows ..........................................................94

 Magical Teas and Washes ............................................96

  Magical Tea ..............................................................97

  Magical Washes.........................................................97

Appendix I  Herbs Listed By Attributes .....................101

 Herbs for Wealth, Abundance, Power, Success, and Prosperity: ............................................................101

 Herbs for Attracting Love and Love Divination:.....101

  Herbs for Lust: ........................................................102

  Herbs for Reversing Love and Lust Magic: .......102

 Herbs for Happiness, Peace, Tranquility, Harmony, and Sleep: .....................................................103

  Herbs for Healing Spells and Health Blessings: 103

  Herbs for Protection and Strength: .....................103

  Herbs for Wishes: ...................................................104

  Herbs for Beauty: ....................................................104

  Herbs for Friendship and Companionship: ........105

 Herbs for Astral Projection, Dreams, and Divination: ....................................................................105

  Herbs for Luck: .......................................................105

  Herbs for Purification and Cleansing: .................105

Appendix II  Recipes.......................................................106

# INTRODUCTION

Thank you for adding this book to your library.
I hope that this reading will be useful to you to start the path towards green magic. In this book you will find a brief history of Wicca and its fundamental elements; an analysis of what the magic of herbs is, what are the main herbs to use and what are their magical properties. You will also find useful tips on how to start practicing magic in everyday life. Finally, I want to thank you with a gift: at the end of this book you will find recipes from my book *The Kitchen Witch*, to bring some magic to your kitchen!

# CHAPTER I

# A BRIEF HISTORY OF WICCA

# The Father of Wicca

The history of Wicca is believed to be filled with mystery and excitement. There are tales of dark nights spent by candle light. Those who follow the Wiccan religion had to hide their beliefs and traditions from around the world. They were forced underground in the Dark Ages by the Church's ever-growing fear of witchcraft and their persecution of Pagans. These are indeed intriguing tales.

It's true that most people are drawn toward the Wiccan religion initially because of these fantastical tales. Some people believe that the origins of Wicca can be traced back as far as the Salem Witch Trials in the New World. However, the actual origins of the Wiccan religion are far more modern.

Modern Wicca's origins can be traced as far back as the mid-20th century. Wicca was founded in England between the 1940s and 1950s by a man named Gerald Gardner. Gerald Gardner became known as the Father of Wicca after he created the very first Wiccan coven and introduced the religion into the modern world.

Gardner was first introduced to occult beliefs and magical practices in Asia. He spent most of his young life there. He also drew some inspiration from reading the writings of Aleister Crowley. He returned to his home in England just before World War II. While in England, Gerald Gardner became involved in the British occult.

In 1954, Gardner published a book titled Witchcraft Today and with the knowledge in this book, he founded his own coven. Gerald Gardner's coven was called the Bricket Wood coven. He formed his religion very quickly. They practiced magic and respected nature as their equal. They believed in the worship of the Goddess, the Horned God, and an assortment of other deities. In Wicca, the female deity was always seen as more powerful and worshiped more than the male. This is probably why the religion gained a lot of ground in modern times, especially among women. Up until the appearance of Wicca in modern times, most other religions are focused on the worship of a male deity. This is why Wicca became gained rapid popularity — because it was different and more appealing to young women.

When Gerald Gardener formed his version of the religion, he changed the way deities were worshipped. He made sure that both the Goddess and the God were seen as equals and worshipped that way. Neither one was more powerful or more important than the other. This was a big change to the religion and it stuck. Even today in modern Wicca, both the God and Goddess are worshiped as equals but some do prefer to choose a favorite out of the deities.

Gardner also never called his religion Wicca. He always referred to his tradition as Witchcraft and later it was known as "The Craft." Some called it "The Old Religion" even though it was not that old. The inspiration for the name 'Wicca' was probably drawn from the word 'Wica' which is an Old English term. It is used to describe sorcerers, witches or people who are skilled in the arts of magic. Gerald Gardner used to refer to the people in his coven as "the Wica," so this is probably where the term Wicca was coined from.

The religion became known as Wicca after it spread to the U.S. and Australia. As Wicca continued to spread from England to the rest of the world, it took on new forms and gathered new traditions. Today there are many different traditions of the Wiccan religion, so those who want to join have plenty of options to choose from.

Some of the different traditions are:

**Gardnerian Wicca**
This is the first and most traditional form of religion. It was named after the Father of Wicca and follows his exact beliefs.

**Alexandrian Wicca**
This is similar to Gardnerian Wicca but was changed a

little to accommodate the New World. This was the first tradition of Wicca to make an appearance in America.

**Dianic Wicca**

This one is popular amongst females and is significantly different from the traditions that came before it. This tradition originated in the U.S. and it focuses only on the worship of the Goddess. Unlike Gerald Gardner's tradition where both the Goddess and God are worshipped as equals, in Dianic Wicca, the Goddess is the main focus and seen as supreme. When it first appeared in the 1970s, it was a female dominant religion and only women were admitted into the covens. However, in modern times both men and women are now allowed to follow the religion and it still focuses on the supremacy of the Goddess.

**Solitary Wicca and Eclectic Wicca**

These are the most popular forms of Wicca today. They are basically Wicca for the solitary and nontraditional witch. Not everyone who follows the tradition has to join a coven or follow a specific tradition. A Solitary Wicca or an Eclectic Wicca can choose what traditions they want to follow and which deities they want to worship. They can mix and match different forms of the tradition to make their own and it allows for more freedom than most religions or traditions.

There are many other forms of Wicca such as **Seax Wicca** or **Celtic Wicca,** but the ones mentioned above are either the most traditional or the more current forms of Wicca. Most newcomers prefer to go the solitary or eclectic route and that is perfectly understandable. It allows you to be free to choose what you believe in instead of forcing you into a stricter and constrained form of worship.

Since its origins, Wicca has gained a lot of ground. It is now a widespread and recognized religion in modern times. It's a spiritual path and a nature centered religion. It's an escape from the modern world filled with concrete jungles and pollution of Earth. That's why Wicca is so popular among young people today.

# The Main Beliefs and Traditions of Modern Wicca

There are many different forms of the Wiccan tradition in modern times. Each tradition has its own beliefs, but there are some core beliefs and traditions that they all follow.

Wicca focuses on creation and the cycle of life and death on Earth. The Goddess and the God are seen the embodiment of the cycle of life and death, and they are the reason for all creation on Earth. Each of the deities govern a part of creation and the existence of everything. It is through the union of the Goddess and the God that life is created and sustained.

The Goddess is associated with the Earth and the Moon. She is the feminine half of the cycle of life and death. She rules over the night sky and the oceans tides through her association with the moon. She is also associated with the reproductive cycle of a woman.

Some traditions of Wicca acknowledge that the Goddess takes on three different forms, also known as the Triple Goddess — the Maiden, the Mother, and the Crone — and each form aligning perfectly with the phases of the Moon.

As the Goddess of Earth, she is associated with the power and strength of physical energy. She is the reason that all life takes root and is allowed to thrive and flourish. She is also associated with our domesticated animals, like cattle and pets, and the fields and crops.

The Goddess is known as both the Mother of God and his partner. Together, they represent the cycle of birth, growth, death, and rebirth. The Goddess is eternal. She never dies. She becomes young, grows old, and then returns to her youthful form, but she is eternal and never dies.

The God is the masculine essence among the deities. He is associated with the Sun. Its light is considered to be associated with the power of male energy and is needed for all life to exist on Earth. The God is also associated with the wild animals of the forest and as well as the hunters. He is often referred to as either the Horned God, to represent the horned animals in the forest, or the Hunter and the Hunted. His job is to protect the animals of the wild from the hunters, but he is also responsible for helping hunters find the food they need to thrive.

In some Wiccan traditions, the God is also represented by other forms. He is associated with the twin gods — the Oak King and the Holly King. These forms of the God represent the changing of the seasons. According to the tradition, the Oak King and the Holly King are brothers who are constantly fighting for the love of the Goddess. They battle each other to see who will win her affection. When the Oak King wins the battle, he rules over the Earth and brings about the seasons of spring and summer. When the Holly King wins the battle, he rules over the Earth during the autumn and winter seasons. When each God wins the battle, the other sleeps through the seasons recovering his strength for the next battle.

The God is not eternal like the Goddess. He is reborn, grows throughout the year, and dies at the end of the year only to be born again. The God is reborn each spring as the Goddess's child. He grows strong throughout the summer becoming the Goddess's partner but then he grows old and dies again each autumn. Then he is reborn again next spring. This is the cycle of life, death, and rebirth.

The co-existence of the Goddess and God is shown in The Wheel of the Year. This is known as the year of the Wiccan religion and shows in detail their holidays and days of worship. In Wicca, there are only eight major holidays known as Sabbats, and each Sabbat represents a cycle of the Gods life, death, and rebirth.

Wiccans also celebrate other holidays known as Esbats. The Esbats are considered to be part of the second Wheel of the Year. An Esbat is celebrated every four weeks when there is a full moon in the night sky. This is when the Wiccan's honor the Goddess for the way she contributes to life and the Earth. Normally, rituals and blessings for the Goddess are held on these days underneath the full moon.

Along with the deities, Wicca also worships or respects the Elements. There are the four classical elements — earth, air, water, and fire — and then in Wicca there is a fifth element known as Spirit. In Wicca, the five elements are seen as being a big part of the cycle of life and death — the creation and existence of all life on Earth. The elements are an important part of Wiccan rituals, traditions, and they are often a part of magical practices and spells.

Another important part of Wicca is the rules they follow. That is the **Wiccan Rede** and the **Threefold Law.** Although most believe that Wicca doesn't actually have any rules, they see these as pieces of advice rather than rules.

The Wiccan Rede is a phrase that most, but not all Wiccans choose to live by. The basic phrase is, "Do what you will as long as it harms none." Most Wiccans choose to follow this because it is seen as the best way to live in harmony with all of existence which is the point of the Wiccan religion.

The Threefold Law, also known as the Rule of Three" co-exists with the Wiccan Rede. It isn't followed by all Wiccans, but it is followed by most. The Threefold Law states that whatever energy you put out into the world returns to you threefold. This is basically seen as a form of karma. If you put negative energy out into the world, it returns to you threefold and the same can be said for positive energy.

This is Modern Wicca.

# CHAPTER II

# THE POWER OF HERBAL MAGIC

# What is Herbal Magic?

Herbal magic has been around for a long time. It was a popular practice long before the formation of Wicca. There was a time when herbal magic and medicine were the same things. Sick people were often healed using herbal concoctions and the healing process was always accompanied by some form of prayer or ritual. This was before the medicine was separated from magic. When the Wiccan religion was formed, herbal magic quickly became a part of its traditions and magical practices.

Wicca is seen as a nature religion. It focuses not just on the worship of nature but working alongside nature and living as its equal. So it would make sense that Wiccans work with herbs in their magical practices.

Plants were living on earth long before humans or animals. It's no surprise that they are believed to have an abundance of power and magic inside them. It's fair to say that herbs and plants are the oldest forms of magic in existence. The origin and survival of herbal magic can be contributed to the practice of shamans, healers of old, and the medicine women and men of the "Old Craft."

Most believe that herbal magic is not only the most powerful form of magic a Wiccan can use, but it is also the most rewarding practice.

Wiccans believe that plants have a certain kind of intelligence and modern science has, in a way, confirmed that belief. Wiccans believe that all plant life actually has consciousness.

Some studies show that plants can and often do communicate and cooperate with each other. Scientists have witnessed plants helping other plants regardless of species. So from the smallest flower to a shrub to even the tallest tree, plants communicate and help each other.

It's mostly seen in a forest or jungle setting where there are many different plants coexisting together. The plants communicate through their roots and forms of fungi. This underground network allows them to transfer nutrients and information to other plants. Let's say that one plant is not getting enough nutrients from sun or rain and another plant has gotten an abundance of nutrients, it will share it with the plant who needs these nutrients. This helps the plant grow even though it's not getting what it needs to survive. It's kind of like borrowing food from each other with the promise of paying it back when it's needed.

Plants also warn or protect each other from threats or danger. If a plant is damaged in any way, then it releases a chemical into the air. This chemical wards off insects and other things that would otherwise harm the plants and warns the other plants of the danger. This is how they protect themselves and other plants from predators like insects.

This evidence of intelligence further shows the power of nature and the magic of Earth. This is why Wiccans choose to tap into the natural magic. Herbal magic is not only the oldest surviving form of magic, but also the most rewarding as it brings you close to the Earth, the Goddess, and the God.

# What is an Herb?

Botanists, herbalists, and other scientists have a specific category for herbs. The plants that fit the category of herb have certain characteristics that make them different from all other plant life. Those who follow Wicca would tell you something else. For Wiccans, healers, witches, and herbalists alike, herbs do not have specific characteristics. In Wicca, an herb is a plant that is useful in any way. This means that whether it's a flower, a weed, a tree, a fruit or vegetable, or even just grass if it has a use or function in Wicca, it's classified as an herb.

Wiccans use all sorts of plants, even deadly and toxic plants. However, the toxic and harmful plants are usually only used by professionals who know exactly how to work with the plant safely. In Wicca, no plant can be seen as good or bad, every plant as its use and is part of the cycle of life and death. When using toxic plants in herbal magic, it is best to heed every warning that comes with it and be as careful as possible.

## The Five Elements in Herbal Magic

Another reason that herbal magic is seen as the most powerful form of Wiccan magic is because of its association with the five elements. Elemental magic has its own form of magic, but it is often intertwined with other forms of magic, especially herbal magic.

It's not difficult to understand the connection the elements have to every part of life. The elements are one of the main reasons that life on Earth exists at all. The same goes for plant life. Herbal magic is made even more magical and powerful through its association with the five elements.

The element of earth shares a connection with herbal magic in several ways. The seed of a plant is used to represent the element earth and it is also planted in the soil of the Earth. The soil nourishes the seed and helps it to grow by lending it energy and power. The plant is not only nourished and fed by the earth, but it is also seen as being a part of the earth itself.

The element fire is connected to herbal magic through the sun. The sun is one of the most powerful representations of the element fire, and without the sun no life can exist. Without the warmth and energy from the sun, a plant cannot grow or live. Earth also helps give plants the energy they need to convert carbon dioxide into oxygen which directly affects the element air.

The element air is connected with herbal magic in a give and take relationship. The plants convert carbon dioxide into oxygen affecting the quality of the air all living creatures breathe. The element air then gives back to the plant by carrying its seeds with the wind to new ground where it can grow new plants and create new life. The air works together with the plant to nourish it and help it grow, and spread its seeds so that the cycle of life continues.

The element water affects herbal magic the same way it affects all living things. Just like all life needs the sun to thrive and exist, the same way, no life can exist on Earth without water. All plants need water to grow and live. The plants don't just take water from the Earth without giving back. Plants are a part of the system that keeps the water table clean. Plants play a crucial role in purifying the water in the Earth and moving it from the soil into the air.

The fifth element known as the Spirit is shown in plants the same way it is shown in everything else. It is their life force, their intelligence, and their will to survive.

There is no better way to show the power of herbal magic than through its connection to the five elements.

## Astrology and Herbs

The planetary bodies in our solar system have played a huge role in civilization ever since humans looked up for the first time. The constellations, the moon, and the sun have played a role in many myths and legends. They also play an important role in many Wiccan beliefs and traditions.

The moon is the embodiment of the Goddess in Wicca and the sun is the embodiment of the God, among other things. The moon, sun, and other parts of our solar system have been used in magic and rituals for centuries. For a very long time in our history, the sun and the moon were the only light that humans had and they were our only means of telling time. It's not hard to believe that many cultures and religions, not just Wicca, used these two heavenly bodies to represent their Gods and Goddesses.

Even today, the sun and the moon still play a vital role in many Wiccan traditions. Astrology is a form of magic itself, often used for divination and connected to herbal magic as well. It is common for those who practice Wicca to combine the power of more than one form of magic to heighten their energy and enhance their power.

All the planets and stars in our solar system have magical correspondence and each one is even connected to certain herbs. Even star signs can be used with its corresponding herbs in magical works. Although the moon's magic is mostly used alongside herbal magic, you can use any part of astrology as long as you feel it has the power you need.

Here is a simple chart explaining the magical correspondents associated with each planetary body used in Wiccan astrology as well as a list of magical herbs that share a connection with that planet:

# Sun (The God)

- **Day**: Sunday
- **Star Sign:** Leo
- In magic, the sun is associated with healing, reason, authority, strength, protection, male energy, divine power, money, prosperity, fire, personal power, purification, and friendships.
- **Herbs**: allspice, almond, cactus, caraway seed, marigold, oak, rosemary, saffron, thyme, sage, orange, cinnamon, chamomile, birch, ash, mistletoe, frankincense, sunflower, rue, Pimpernel, oats, hops, daisies, buttercups, alfalfa, banana, citron, pineapple, tarragon, etc.

# Moon (The Goddess)

- **Day**: Monday
- **Star Sign:** Cancer
- In magic, the moon is associated with dreams, family, medicine, spiritual growth, intuition, the ocean, love, fertility, passion, death, rebirth, mystery, and the afterlife.
- **Herbs**: aloe, apple, Adder's tongue, ash, angelica, coconut, cedar, clary sage, clevers, lemon, lemon grass, lemon balm, honeysuckle, grapes, cucumber, dill, jasmine, mushroom, mugwort, maple, magnolia, mistletoe, sesame seed, spearmint, turnip, moonflower, water lily, white oak, white rose, wormwood, witch hazel, willow, peach, parsley, milkweed, cedar, pear, yew, etc.

# Mercury

- **Day**: Wednesday
- **Star Sign:** Virgo and Gemini
- In Wicca, Mercury is not usually associated with a God that is commonly shared but in magic, it does have certain associations. It's associated with divination, communication, self-improvement, and insight.
- **Herbs**: alfalfa, carrots, cedar, almond, fennel, lavender, lungwort, caraway, cedar, fern, hazel, parsnips, honeysuckle, sage, walnut, parsley, peppermint, dill, mace, oats, pecan, slippery elm, skullcap, etc.

## *Venus*

- **Day**: Friday
- **Star sign**: Libra and Taurus
- Venus also doesn't have a common association with a God in Wicca. In magic, it is associated with love, pleasure, fertility, and art.
- **Herbs**: basil, apple, cherry, African violet, daisies, cocoa, daffodils, alder, ash, catnip, apple, fern, jasmine, lime, orchid, pear, parsley, juniper, celery, cumin, lily of the valley, strawberry, violet, wheat, thyme, vanilla, rose, radish, plum, primrose, elder, foxglove, etc.

## *Mars*

- **Day**: Tuesday
- **Star sign**: Aries
- In magic, this planet is associated with hunting, courage, competitions, physical strength, logic, and war.
- **Herbs**: allspice, cherry, bloodroot, chili pepper, male fern, honeysuckle, ginger, hawthorn, pine, red oak, red rose, thistle, wormwood, rue, tarragon, beets, cherry, cashews, bleeding heart, hemlock, holly, etc.

## *Saturn*

- **Day**: Saturday
- **Star sign**: Capricorn
- Saturn is mostly associated with karma and meditation. In magic, it is associated with change, motivation, understanding, death, banishing, and reincarnation. However, when Saturn is in retrograde,

it is associated with slowing down time, delays, disappointments, mistakes, testing patience, and karmic retribution. It is wise to refrain from magic work when Saturn is in retrograde.
- **Herbs**: comfrey, monkshood, hemlock, cornflower, elder, fern, elm, rue, skullcap, nightshade, tobacco, witch hazel, cypress, garlic, knotweed, myrrh, patchouli, tamarind, pine, etc.

## *Jupiter*

- **Day**: Thursday
- **Star sign**: Sagittarius
- Jupiter is associated with dedication, loyalty, endurance, luck, money, and faithfulness.
- **Herbs**: cedar, lungwort, jasmine, juniper, milk thistle, lavender, wallflower, mistletoe, lilac, violet, agrimony, chestnut, lemon, cinnamon, hyssop, dandelion, milkweed, sage, etc.

## The Magic of the Moon

In Wicca, the moon is seen as the most powerful object in our solar system. It is associated with the Goddess and has many magical connections. In many Wiccan traditions, their spell work and rituals surround the rise and fall, and the different phases of the moon. The moon is even honored every full moon on the Wiccan calendar.

In magical practices, Wiccans like to plan their magical works, spell casting, and rituals around the moon cycles. For example, if you wish to do magic that will directly affect you, then you can wait until the moon is in the right position to affect your star sign before performing your spell. There are many other ways as well to use the magic of the moon in your practices.

Wiccans tend to use the different phases of the moon to cast their spells. Each phase the moon goes through has a meaning and a certain level of power. You can time your magic with the phases of the moon in order to get the exact results you desire. Moon magic and herbal magic are both complicated, but extremely rewarding.

Here is a simple chart to help you time your magic with the moon's phases:

## New Moon

This is the very beginning of the moon cycle. It is best to use this phase in the moon cycle to perform magic intended to start or bring new things into your life.

Anything involving attracting something new that you want in your life will perform well during this phase of the moon cycle.

## Waxing Moon

This phase of the moon can be utilized by putting action or directing energy toward your goals. You can use the magic from this moon to strengthen the relationships in your life or take big steps towards your other goals.

This part of the moon cycle is strongly associated with action and direction.

So this is the best time to take action in your life and move forward. Send your intentions out into the universe and don't be afraid to take action knowing that the magic of the moon will back you up.

## Full Moon

This phase of the moon is honored and worshiped every four weeks. This time is known as an Esbat in Wicca. The full moon is the most powerful phase in the moon cycle.

Wiccans believe that the full moon is the best time to perform any spell work as any intention will be favored by the moon's power. Therefore, most Wiccans try to save any of their spells and magic for the full moon.

## Waning Moon:

This is the start of the end of the cycle. This is the best time to release any energy outward into the universe. Spells intended to attract or bring new things to you will not be successful during this time. You will want to use this time to expel negative energy from your life and get over any negative experiences. Spells and magical work aimed at resolving issues and conflicts, overcoming obstacles and illnesses will be the most successful.

## Dark Moon:

This is the end of the cycle and will occur only days before the cycle repeats itself and we arrive at the new moon again. The dark moon is associated with negative energy and its magic is known for having destructive potential. Most Wiccans try to restrain from performing any magic related to the moon during this time as it could have consequences or a karmic nature. This can repercussions that you normally would not expect.

Wiccans prefer to use this time to renew and refresh their inner energy as well as expel any excess negative energy. This is a time for replenishing and refreshing. You should use this time to prepare yourself for the next new moon.

Herbal magic and astrology almost go hand and hand. Wiccans mostly use the sun and the moon in their magical practices, but there's nothing stopping you or anyone using all of astrology. If you can find the right way to harness the magic of the universe, then, by all means, use it.

Moon magic is the most common component in herbal

magic. You can even make a moon garden for your herbs so they are empowered by the magic of the moon while they are growing. The sun empowers every plant, so it's easy to use the sun in your herbal magic. It sounds complicated but the rewards both in the energy and magic you receive are worth the work you need to put into it.

# CHAPTER III

# WORKING WITH HERBS

# WORKING WITH HERBS

When it comes to working with herbs, it may be easy to just look at a list of herbs you need and head straight to the store. Buying ready-to-use herbs may be easier but when it comes to herbal magic, it's not the best choice. Homegrown is always best.

Wiccans have a very simple reason for this. Magical works and spell casting is all about using and directing the energy that is available to you in the universe. There is magical energy ready to be used all around us and within us. The reason most Wiccans prefer to grow their own herbs for magical works is that it gives them an opportunity to direct energy into the herbs and make them even more powerful.

While growing and maintaining a garden of your own, you can direct your personal energy into the plant while it is growing. You may already have an idea or plan for this particular plant so you can direct a specific energy into the plant for better long term yield and use.

If you choose to buy the herbs you need for magical work, they will still contain natural energy and power. However, their potential will never be properly realized because there wasn't an opportunity to direct further energy into the herbs while they were growing. You can try directing your energy into the herbs after you buy them but it won't have as great an impact. Store-bought herbs may have soaked up the energy of whoever grew them, which isn't always the best thing. Perhaps, the person who grew them felt sick or had really low energy for reasons known to them, and as a result, they may have inadvertently directed negative energy into the herbs as they were growing. No matter what you're using the herbs for, if they have any kind of negative energy in them, it can seriously harm you or your intentions for the herbs.

Growing and maintaining your own witch's garden may seem like a lot more work than it actually is. There are simple steps and tricks you can use to make it easier. You can grow your own herbs indoors and outdoors. As long as you're willing to put the work in you won't regret it.

# A WITCH'S GARDEN

Creating a witch's garden is a rewarding and fun task. You can create a witch's garden from scratch or even transform an existing garden so it has that witchy feel and look. It doesn't matter if you have a large outdoor space or a small indoor or outdoor space, you will still be able to design a witch's garden no matter the amount of space available to you.

There are several types of gardens, however, what your garden looks like and represents will depend on the kind of magic you want to practice. A witch's garden also doesn't need to have an exact theme. You can mix and match different themes depending on your preferences. You can even make up your own theme as you go along.

The one thing to remember is that your witch garden should be a place to use for rituals, meditation, peace, and healing. It's a place you should be able to go to at any time and just relax and soak up all that magical energy while giving some of your own energy back to the garden.

## The Makings of a Witch's Garden

A witch's garden allows for expression and freedom. It can be whatever you want it to be. It can contain any plants you want it to. It can represent anything you want it to represent.

However, on the large scale of things, there are a few objects and tools that you should have and steps that you should take in order for your garden to thrive. The choice is yours, but some of these objects are a must-have for a Wiccan who wants to excel in the realm of herbal magic.

### Add a Garden Altar

Altars are an important part of Wicca. It is usually in the center of rituals, magical work, and spell casting. There are also different kinds of altars. You can have a permanent altar, a temporary altar, but mostly an altar is an extremely personal object.

Having an altar in the garden can have many uses. You can use it to meditate within the garden which would make it easier for you to direct your energy and magic into the plants around you. You can also use the same altar for your harvesting rituals when you harvest the herbs you need for your magical works. You can also choose to use the same altar for any rituals or spell casting you have in mind.

It's common for Wiccans to have more than one altar. So if you choose, you can have an altar in your garden specifically for meditating, directing energy, and harvesting. Then you can have a separate altar inside your house or anywhere else, and use that altar for magical works and spells.

Putting an altar in your garden is a personal choice. You can put it wherever you want. It can be made out of whatever you want. You can place whatever you want on it. However, given that this is a witch's garden altar there are a few tips you should keep in mind when designing it.

1. A garden altar should be made out of natural things. Try using natural rocks or boulders with a flat surface so it can act as a table. If it has moss on it, that's even better. You could also consider a tree stump for an altar. It would be better if the tree stump was planted in the ground so its roots were allowed to grow into the soil. A tree stump can be treated so that it's still alive, but not able to grow anymore. For a garden altar, the more natural items that are used to build it, the better it is.

2. Make sure you cleanse not only the altar but the place you plan to place it at before you continue. Cleansing or smudging the object and the area will repeal any

negative energy. This will ensure that your magical works and rituals won't be interrupted or ruined by any unwanted energy.

3. You can place your altar anywhere you want, but it would be better if you can place it directly in the middle of the garden. If you're using this place for meditation, directing energy or any kind of magical work, it is better that it be placed in the center of the garden. This ensures the even distribution of any magical energy throughout the entire garden. This also means that whenever you're at your altar, you will be completely surrounded by the magical energy from your garden.

Consider placing items on or around your altar that correspond with the theme of the garden you want. An elemental garden requires elemental objects and a moon garden requires things that are associated with the moon. If you don't have an exact theme, don't stress, there are only a few things you need to have on your altar. The tools you use to harvest the herbs from your garden should be kept on the altar in the garden. Cleansing tools and objects should be kept nearby. Something personal of yours to maintain your personal energy in the garden must be added. There are plenty more, but these are the most important objects that should be kept on your garden altar.

### Choose Your Plants Wisely

When you first start planning your garden, you need to put a lot of thought into the herbs you want to plant in your garden. Given that there are a lot of variables to consider, it is best to sit down and visualize and think about the garden you want. Once you're sure of what you want — the kind of garden, the theme, and the herbs you want to plant — start by listing the herbs that correspond with your plan.

Along with the theme of your garden, there are several other reasons to carefully list the herbs you'll be planting.

1. You need to know for certain what kind of spells and magical works you will be performing. Herbs are only associated with a few things and they are only used in certain spells. You can't perform a love spell if you don't have any herbs that are associated with love. So if you're unsure of the kind of magic you will be practicing, ensure that you plant a wide variety of herbs you can use for any occasion.

2. Insects are friends. I know you may not want bees and other insects flying around your garden, but for a witch's garden, this is a good thing. Insects are a part of nature and although some of them can harm your garden, most of them can help it grow. You can control what insects you attract and how many of them you attract through planting the right herbs.

You can plant bee-friendly herbs in small sections around the garden. This will attract a small number of bees that pollinate your plants and bring good energy into your garden. There are also certain plants you can have in your garden that will keep unwanted insects — the type that harms your garden — away. It's all about balance. You need to find a balance between nature and your garden.

3. Plan the layout of your herbs before you start planting them. Some herbs will grow well when they are planted beside each other, while other herbs will overgrow and consume the space of any herbs near them. Before you start the planting process, find out which plants can grow together and which ones need their own space, and then plan the layout of your garden.

### **Invite Nature into Your Garden**

Your garden is a part of nature. At least you want it to be. Herbal magic and the Wiccan religion are about being close to nature. Working alongside nature, protecting nature, and respecting nature is a part of the Wiccan life.

You have a garden now and you grow and care for the herbs you use in your magic. You are giving back to nature through the plants you are growing. It is a lovely give and takes relationship. Let your garden become a true part of nature and not just another section of your house.

Invite the natural creatures of the world into your garden. You're probably already doing this with the bees and other insects, but don't stop there. Make your garden a sanctuary for other animals. Hang some bird feeders and bird houses in your garden. You can even add a lovely bird pond that matches the theme of your garden.

There are plenty of animals you can invite into your garden without worrying about them making a mess or bringing unwanted energy. You just need to do some research and put some thought and intention into it.

By inviting animals into your garden, you make your garden a true part of nature. Even if you have an indoor garden or if you do not have a large outdoor space, you can still hang up a birdhouse or two. There are lots of ways you can make your garden a part of nature. If you do this, you will bring in a new, powerful energy that will be given to you by the animals you invite into your garden. This can make your herbs more powerful than you can imagine.

### Leave Your Water In The Moonlight

You should set up a watering schedule. It's best to water your garden during the day or depending on the instructions given to you with each seed. Watering your plants is one of the times you get to pour your energy and intentions into them. Another way you can empower plants with healing and positive energy is through the water you use on them.

Try filling your watering can with water at the end of the day, when the sun has already set and the moon is out. Leave the watering can outside underneath the moonlight all night long. During the night, the water will warm to a nice temperature for the plants, as they don't like really cold tap water, and the water would have soaked up energy from the moon. By the time you need to go outside and water your plants, the water will already be infused with the magical energy of the moon and that energy will be transferred to your plants.

Don't leave your watering can out at night during the Dark Moon phase. This could bring potentially harmful energy to your plants.

### Set up a Schedule

The only way your garden will thrive is when you have established a proper schedule for its care and maintenance — a schedule for planting, maintaining, watering, and harvesting. There are a few ways you can do this.

Most folks try to set a schedule that works well with their day to day life so they can easily work around their garden. Some try to do it in a magical way to ensure their garden is infused with magical energy at every possible moment. You can set your schedule based on the respective phases of the moon to bring forth energy from the moon into your garden and your life. Set a schedule that works best for you and do your best not to stray from it. This is necessary to ensure your garden thrives.

Ensure that your schedule involves spending some time in your garden every day. This should be to meditate or care for the plants. You can use this time to direct your energy into your plants every day.

### Keep it All Natural

In order to completely align with the power of nature, you need to keep your garden as natural as possible. That means using all natural ingredients and objects. Your compost and soil should be as natural as possible. You shouldn't use any insecticides or chemicals to keep away unwanted creatures. It needs to be in harmony with nature.

There are natural insecticides you can use. Even some

plants act as insecticides so try to use any natural way you can and avoid unnatural chemicals. Some compost can have artificial ingredients that ensure healthy and strong growing plants, but it's best to avoid those. You can get natural soil for your garden and even make your own natural compost by recycling old food. Comfrey tea is great for feeding your plants and there are plenty of homemade compost recipes you can follow.

Dead leaves that have fallen from trees are usually seen as an eyesore and raked away. These leaves can make good natural compost for your garden. They need to be shredded in order to speed up the decomposing process. Mix the shredded dead leaves with coffee grounds to get the decomposing process going. Leaves turn into good mulch all by themselves, but it takes a number of years for them to decompose fully. You need to add something that is rich in nitrogen to help the leaves break down. Once you've mixed the leaves and coffee grounds together, simply add water and add it to your soil.

This is one of many different natural composts you can use to keep your garden as natural as possible.

## Themes for a Witch's Garden

### An Elemental Garden

Elemental magic is different from herbal magic. Having an elemental garden makes complete sense as the elements play such a huge role in the growth and maintenance of plant life. An elemental theme is perfect as the elements are not only powerful, but they are an integral part of a plant's growth process. By honoring the elements with your garden, you will harness their magic and empower your plants.

To honor the elements in your garden, place elemental objects in the directions associated with each element: north, south, east, and west. The elements are often associated with the directions on the compass, so keep these directions in mind when placing your elemental objects.

Fire is associated with the South. Air is associated with the East. Water is associated with the West. Earth is associated with the North. You should place your altar in the center of the garden so it acts as a focal point for the elements. You can also turn your altar, or the focal point, into the fifth element, spirit, using certain objects.

## *Fire*

Fire can be represented by objects, colors, magical tools, and certain plants. To represent fire in your elemental garden, start by planting flowers and herbs that represent fire in the southern corner of your garden.

Plants that represent fire are basil, rosemary, marigold, holly, dill, fennel, red sunflowers, and coriander to name a few. Plant herbs like these in the southern corner to represent fire.

You can also use objects to represent fire in your elemental garden. Candles are a tool used in elemental spells and also a representation of the fire element. You can place candles in safe places along the southern corner of your garden. Make sure they are in places where the wax would drip onto any plants should you decide to light the candles.

This way the flame won't burn or damage anything nearby. Fire is often represented by the colors red and gold. Items such as ribbons or crystals of these colors can be scattered or hung around the southern direction of the garden to further represent the element fire.

Tools that represent fire on your altar are usually the Athame or any dagger. So make sure you keep this on your garden altar at all times.

## Air

Air is associated with the East so it should be represented on the east side of your garden. You can represent air by using colors, objects, plants, and tools throughout the eastern section of your garden.

Plants that are associated with air are caraway, lavender, sage, mint, parsley, and broom to name a few. Plant these and other herbs in the eastern corner of your garden to represent air.

The objects you can use to represent air are simple. There is already air all around you which already plays a role in your elemental garden. Simple objects like old Chinese hand-fans are a simple way to further represent air. You could also hang some wind chimes around the eastern corner of your garden and maybe place a small windmill somewhere as well. Air is associated with the color yellow. Some yellow ribbons hung around the eastern corner are a good idea.

As for tools, the witch's wand or staff is usually used to represent air in spells and magical works. Keep a wand or staff on your garden altar.

## Earth

Earth is associated with the North so you can represent it on the northern side of your elemental garden.

Plants associated with the element earth are honeysuckle, tulips, bulbs, magnolia, and quince to name a few. You can plant herbs like this and others in the northern corner of your garden.

Earth, just like air, is already represented throughout your whole garden. It is represented through the soil and the seeds you plant in the soil as well as the plant life all around you. The only thing you need to do now is to focus the energy of the element on the north side of the garden.

Salt is a common object used to represent earth in

spells and rituals. You can sprinkle some salt around the north corner or you can keep a bowl of salt near or on your altar. The pentagram also symbolizes the earth, so you can keep that on your altar or hang it in the northern corner of the garden. The color green is associated with earth along with other dark 'earthy' colors. Some green ribbons or crystals can be scattered or hung around the north end of the garden.

## *Water*

Water is associated with the West so you can represent it in the western section of your garden. You honor water every time you water the plants in your garden but there are other ways to honor it in your garden.

One of the best ways to represent water in your garden is with a water feature. This can be a pond or fountain, any kind of water feature in the west of your garden. You can make it as beautiful and natural as you want. It adds a certain feeling to the garden and makes it look that much more magical.

Plants that are associated with water are water lilies, aloe, daisy, watercress, Himalayan poppy, and foxglove to name a few. Plant these in the west corner of your garden. Some plants like water lilies can even be allowed to grow in your water feature if you choose to have one.

Water is associated with the colors blue and white so you can hang ribbons or scatter crystals of those colors around the West side of your garden. The tools that are often used to represent water are chalices, bowls, and cauldrons, usually filled with water and left on your altar.

If you love the idea of any elemental garden but you don't want to represent all the elements at once, you can have a single element garden. You can have a garden that is fully dedicated to just one element if you want. Either way, the choice is all yours.

## A Moon Garden

With a moon garden, you will use your entire garden to represent and honor the moon. The moon is a magical symbol in Wicca. It is one of the embodiments of the Goddess and is a very powerful symbol. By having a moon garden you will use mostly moon associated plants and you will probably only be working in the garden during night time.

The plants used in your moon garden will represent the moon through their color or by blooming at night. You can add other plants but there should only be a few of them and they should be scattered around to accent the other plants. If they are too close together their colors may be overwhelming and ruin the feel of the moon garden.

The moon is associated with the colors grey and silver. Only plant plants that share the same color. Night-blooming and night-scented plants should also be added to your garden. Plants like moonflowers, white roses, night-scented orchids, night-blooming jasmine, Shasta daisies, night-scented stock, dusty miller, mugwort, lavender, wormwood, dianthus, and white lilies. Keep in mind, if you are planting lilies, however, they are poisonous to cats — the petals, leaves, stems, and even the pollen is harmful to cats so if you have a cat then you should avoid planting lilies of any kind.

When planting your garden, try placing the plants in a circular pattern with your altar in the center and paths along the sides leading to the altar. This will symbolize the full moon, but it is not necessary. You can also place the plants in smaller circles around the garden to represent the full moon.

Your altar doesn't need to be in the center of the garden when it comes to a moon garden. Instead, you can add a circular pond to the center of your garden. This can catch the moon's light and reflect it as well as be a representation of the full moon itself.

Ideally, you will want your moon garden to be outdoors so that it can bathe in the moon's glow whenever the moon is out. The way you've arranged the plants will determine whether or not they will be able to catch the moon's light and reflect it. This is why you should ensure you scatter the non-moon associated plants properly.

Other ways to represent the moon in your moon garden is through decoration. You can get glowing rocks and scatter them around the garden. There are some natural lights that glow in the dark which you can also add those to your moon garden. You can also add stepping stones throughout your garden as a path and paint them with something that glows in the dark. Orbs are also a nice touch. Moon symbols or placing things in a moon shape should also be considered. When decorating your moon garden, make sure that whatever you add does not outshine the natural glow of the moon or the plants.

Another thing you should remember about a moon garden is that your harvesting and planting rituals need to be planned around the moon cycles. You need to know the best phase of the moon for planting new flowers, the phase of the moon for harvesting, and the phase of the moon needed for clearing and renewing the ground for new seeds.

The New Moon is a good time to clear the ground of old plants and refresh and renew the soil. You'll want to use this phase of the moon to cleanse the area. This is the perfect time to make an area ready to plant new seeds.

The Waxing Moon is perfect for taking action toward a goal, so use the time to plant new seeds in your garden. Also, use it to care for and water the plants you already have. You can also use this time to harvest if you choose.

The Full Moon is the best phase for harvesting your herbs and performing any magical work. You can use the full moon for mostly anything however. You can plant new seeds, clear old ground and cleanse it, and maintain and care for your plants. The Full Moon is usually accepting of all activities, but it is the best phase of the moon to harvest your herbs and perform some magic.

The Waning Moon can be used to cleanse the whole

garden of any unwanted or negative energy that made its way in. You can also use this time to care for the garden and meditate at your altar. Try and use this time to fill the garden and plants with as much of your energy as you can. Also, soak in the energy for yourself.

During the Dark Moon, it is best to keep away from your garden. The dark moon can bring negative energy with it so it's better to stay out of the garden during night time. Try to water and care for the plants during the day and do not leave any water outside underneath the moon.

### Astrological Garden

There are several ways you can design an astrological garden. You'll want to use plants that are connected to the sun, the moon, the star signs, and other planetary bodies. You can make a garden that is dedicated to all of these or only some of them. You can represent all the star signs in your garden or just your star sign in particular.

If you choose to represent all the star signs, one design you could create is an astrology wheel in your garden. Make a circle with shape in a section of your garden. This can be the center of your garden around your altar or anywhere else. The wheel should have 12 sections to represent all of the star signs. In each section place plants that represent the specific star sign in that section.

- For **Aries**, plant tulips, sage, hollyhock, stinging nettle, and more.
- For **Gemini**, plant lilac, lavender, lily of the valley, lemon balm, yarrow, and more.
- For **Leo**, plant sunflowers, fennel, marigold, chamomile, St. John's wort, and more.
- For **Taurus**, plant rose, lily, thyme, daisy, and more.
- For **Cancer**, plant poppy, white rose, passion flower, water lily, mugwort, and more.
- For **Scorpio**, plant sage, marigold, wormwood, and more.
- For **Virgo**, plant mint, jasmine, rosemary, skullcap,

buttercup, and more.
- For **Capricorn**, plant hemlock, black poppy, coltsfoot, pansy, vervain, and more.
- For **Libra**, plant foxglove, marjoram, and more.
- For **Aquarius**, plant peppermint, lavender, and more.
- For **Sagittarius**, plant hellebore, rosemary, juniper, narcissus, and more.
- For **Pisces**, plant iris, thyme, water lilies, tarragon, violets, and more.

If you don't want to represent all the star signs in your garden, you only need to represent yours or anyone else who lives in the home with you. You also don't need to place the plants in a circle. You can scatter them around the garden or section them off so you know which plant belongs to which star sign. You can also mark each star sign with an actual sign. You can make this yourself and it can be the name of the star sign, the symbol, or even the constellation associated with the star sign.

You can decorate your astrological garden anyway you want — with star symbols, sun symbols, and moon symbols. You can hang carvings of the sun, stars, and moon all around the garden. You can place stepping stones in certain shapes to represent the moon, sun, or stars.

You can even represent other planets in your garden. However you want to decorate your astrological garden is up to you.

# A Witch's Garden For All Spaces and Situations

Some people are lucky enough to have a big outdoor space in their backyard or in front of their house. This is great if you want to start a witch's garden. However, some people might only have a small patio, balcony, or no outdoor space at all and they probably don't think they can have a witch's garden. The best part about a witch's garden is that it doesn't matter how much space you have or what your current situation is, you can make yourself a witchy garden no matter what. Even if you already have a garden and you want it to be more witchy. That's as easy as doing a little decorating.

## Witching up an Existing Garden

We'll start with the easy steps. If you already have a garden, indoors or outdoors, it's quite easy to turn it into a witch's garden. The difference between an ordinary garden and a witch's garden is in the feeling you get from it. You should be able to feel the magical energy floating through the air. You should feel as if you are one with nature. The best way to get this feeling from your witch garden is by adding things that are covered in magical energy and most importantly your own personal energy.

With an existing garden, it's not too late to pick a theme and add things that correspond with that theme. No matter what theme you choose, there are a few things that you can add to make your garden have a witchy feel.

1. You should add a **Garden Altar** to your garden. This is easy. Your altar can be whatever you want it to be and you can put it wherever you want. Traditionally, the altar is placed in the center of the garden but this isn't a hard rule. You should try and match your altar to the theme you've picked for your garden and have the essential tools on or around it.

2. You can place **colorful crystals** around your garden. Crystals are very magical tools used in Wiccan spells and magic. They can also hold energy very well. Get a few crystals, (if you have a theme for your garden, then get corresponding colored crystals), and fill them with energy. You can meditate at your garden altar and direct your

energy into the crystals, then scatter them around your garden.

3. **Witchy symbols** are great for decorating your garden. You can get things like carved wooden moons, suns, and stars to hang up. You can get a witchy broom like you see on T.V. and place that somewhere or hang it up. Wind chimes and dream catchers are considered to be quite magical, so go ahead and hang some of those up. Anything that you think will make your garden feel witchy can be added. It's all up to you.

4. **Candles** are a great source of magical energy and they can also hold your energy. Try getting some candles and placing them around the garden. If you can incorporate it, have some artistic, wooden candle holders as well. Once again if you have a theme then you should try getting corresponding colors for your candles. Be careful that you don't place them anywhere flammable.

5. Of course, you can always add more magical plants and herbs to your garden. Your garden may already be filled with flowers and herbs of all sorts, but you can always add more. You may have planted those seeds before you knew what kind of power they held. Perhaps you want more herbs for love or wealth. By all means, plant those herbs and make the most out of the space you have.

## Utilizing a Large Space for a Witch's Garden

It's the best when you have a large space to work with. If you have a big garden at the back of your home or in the front, you can basically do whatever you want. The more space you have, the more freedom you have. You can go all out with the decorations, the plants, and the themes.

One of the problems you might face, however, is with your neighbors. Not everyone will be accepting of a Wiccan and it's understandable if you would prefer to keep your witchy ways a secret from the neighborhood. You may face this problem if you can only utilize a front garden if you don't have a lot of privacy in your front or back garden. There are lots of ways you can have your witchy garden while avoiding any possible ridicule from the people around you.

### **Privacy**

This is a thing we all strive for and there are plenty of ways to reach this goal. However, big walls and fences may make you feel like you're in prison. You can get the privacy you want without having to surround your garden with high brick walls or big metal fences that block out the sun and separate you from the world. You can use your garden and nature itself to give you the kind of privacy you need.

Tall hedges are a nice addition to any garden. They don't need to be so tall that they block out the sunlight. They just need to be tall enough so nobody can stand on their tiptoes and peer into your garden. This is a nice way to keep your garden as natural as possible while still maintaining your privacy. You can even go for flowery hedges to add a touch of color to your garden wall.

Trees and thick foliage are also a form of privacy. You can surround your garden with tall trees and some thick foliage. Plant a different tree on each corner of your garden. Trees take longer to grow so this won't be an immediate solution to your privacy problem, but you can get fully grown trees transported to your garden and planted there. The trees should be tall with a thick trunk and lots of leaves. Additionally, you can add some thick bushes or foliage to cover up the rest of the space.

Lavender tends to grow fairly thick and bushy so you could surround your garden with lavender and let it grow freely. Then plant the rest of your garden in the middle. You can also scatter a few white fences around the outside of your garden and let vines grow up them. These will great a natural and beautiful wall.

Of course, if you don't care about your neighbors seeing your witchy garden, then go ahead and do whatever you want.

### **Wrap-around Garden**

If you are lucky enough to have a garden both in front and behind your house then you are in a great position. Take the opportunity to utilize all the space you have. You can create a wrap-around garden. In other words, you can create a witch's garden in such a way that it wraps around your house.

You can make a wheel of the year garden that circles around your house. You can do the same with an astrology wheel. You can also expand on an elemental theme by using all four corners of both your front and back garden.

You are also lucky enough to have a lot of space to plant as many different herbs as you want. Wrap-around gardens are great and it's definitely something to consider if you are in the position to have one.

The most important thing to remember is that your garden is yours. If you have a large space for your witch's garden, don't hold yourself back. Go wild. Do whatever you want and just make the space your own. Use as much or as little of the space as you want to.

Get creative with your garden creation and don't hold yourself back. It doesn't matter what theme you want, don't be afraid to use it. Create a maze in your garden using your herbs. Go online and look for inspiration. Do whatever you want and have fun with it.

### **Creating a Small Witch's Garden**

You may have little to no space outside or inside your house but that doesn't mean you can't have a witchy garden. Technically, it isn't an actual garden. However, when it comes to a witch's garden, it can be anything inside or outside. You don't have to jump through hoops to make yourself a witch's garden, all you have to do is get a little creative.

In this modern world filled with concrete jungles, most of us live in apartment buildings. This means that we are lucky if we have so much as a balcony for our outdoor space. Even if you live in a house, you may have a small courtyard for a garden or a simple patio. Today is all about minimalism, so nice big gardens are a rare sight. All you need is a bit of creativity and time to turn whatever space you have into a witchy garden filled with magic and herbs.

Thankfully, many of the herbs and plants used in herbal magic can be grown in pots. So if you don't have an actual garden, don't worry, there is always a solution.

### A Patio or Balcony Garden

You can turn your balcony or patio space into a beautiful witch's garden. You can decorate the space with witchy symbols, candles, crystals, wind chimes, and more. This is all about being creative with what you have.

It might be a good idea to install some wooden shelves if you have space for them outside. The wooden shelves can expand the small space and allow you to add more herbs. You can place the shelves along a wall, hang them from the ceiling or just add normal shelves to the space so you can stack your pots. Wood shelves are the best if you're looking for a natural and witchy feel. Another option would be smooth stone shelves.

For your garden altar, you may need to use a temporary altar rather than a permanent one. Since you are limited with the amount of space you have, it's best to have a makeshift altar instead of a permanent one. You would have to work around the altar and it would make your everyday routine harder than it needs to be.

Temporary garden altars are simple. You can place a clean cloth on the ground, this can be any color that you choose, but white is usually the traditional choice. Next, place a small pillow in front of the cloth for you to sit or kneel on. Now place your tools on the cloth and your altar is ready. This is the best option for small spaces. You can put it down when you want to use it and then pick it up and put it aside when you're not around.

You can also decorate your pots to make them have a witchy feel. You can tie a ribbon around the brim of the pot. The color of the ribbon can correspond with the use of the plant inside the pot. You can also place crystals with specific colors near or inside some of the pots. Another option for the shelves is to use them to hold candles. You can also hang candles from the ceiling using thin chains and small hooks.

When it comes to any small area, the more creative you are the better the space is going to be. In the end it's all about how you feel in your garden. If it has a witchy feeling and you feel like you're close to nature, then you've done a good job.

## A Small Courtyard Garden

I once lived in a house that had an outdoor space, but it was just a courtyard. There were bricks laid out on the floor and it was surrounded by a high brick wall. Although, it got ample sunshine, the bricks made it feel and look cold. The high wall might have provided some privacy and protection, but it made me feel trapped and cut off. These types of outdoor spaces are common in big cities, however, but there are simple steps to take to make it into an amazing and witchy space.

The first thing to do is make that brick wall more inviting. You can nail some white or wooden fences to the wall and get some vine plants to grow up and around them. This will instantly turn a brick wall into a beautiful homemade hedge. Vine plants grow fast but they won't grow over night so you have to be patient and keep your mind set on the end result.

You can 'witch' up the remainder of the space using decoration and creativity. You can use plants potted in big and small pots and arrange them any way you like. Remember you can also get creative and decorate the pots. You can also ditch the pots and get wooden planters to add a more witchy and natural feel. A nice water feature in the corner of the courtyard will tie the whole thing together.

You can add some natural light at night by adding some shelves and placing candles on them. You can also create a metal or stone burner in the center or in the corner of the courtyard. The burner can be used for a small, controlled bonfire. For a witchy look and feel you can hang a cauldron over the burner.

Your altar can be set next to the burner or anywhere you want. A courtyard is small, but it probably has more space than a patio or balcony. If you want a permanent altar, then you can create a beautiful one in this space. However, if you prefer the temporary altar so you can make the most of your small space then that is your choice.

Once again be as creative as you want to be. That is the best way to create a witch's garden.

### Indoor Garden

As a last resort, even if you have absolutely no outdoor space to work with, you can create your garden inside your house. Everybody has houseplants. You can choose magical houseplants that won't take up too much space in your home, yet still, be used for herbal magic.

Once again, decorate the pots in order to make them feel witchy. A nice way to decorate indoor pots is by creating a miniature fairy garden. This means that you make each pot look like a garden for a tiny fairy. One of my favorite designs is a fairy house. To do this, you need to get some small toys and some glass planters.

Fill the glass jars or planters with a little bit of soil, just below half of the planter. The toys you would get would be small objects you can use to make a house. A tiny door or a small house would be great, maybe even a small mailbox or chairs. Basically you want things from a dollhouse. Use these toys to create a makeshift tiny garden in the glass planter. For example, you can take a mound of soil and press a toy door against the soil. Cover the top of the soil and around the door with green moss to make it look like grass. Then plant some sprigs of lavender or mint to make it look like a tree of bushes near the toy door. Add some small pebbles in front of the door so they look like stepping stones. Now you have a small fairy garden growing a tree of lavender or a bush of mint. The end result should resemble a small house inside a grassy hill with some stepping stones in front of a tiny door and a lovely lavender tree or mint bush beside it.

You can make this design and many others like it, both indoors and outdoors. This is a great way to have a witch's garden inside and out.

It's a good idea to try and set up your indoor altar near where you grow the bulk of your plants. This way your altar can double as an indoor altar and a garden altar. You can also just place your plants around your altar if it already exists, instead of moving them back and forth.

Last but not least, you need to pick your plants carefully. Not all plants can survive indoors, nor are all indoor plants are very magical or useful. There are a few magical herbs that will thrive indoors so you just need to be wary of that when creating your indoor garden.

Here is a short and simple list of magical indoor plants: orchids, aloe, Chinese money plant, African violets, spider plants, etc.

There are also plenty of plants that can survive with little to no sun: chives, mint, foxglove, parsley, lemon balm, cilantro, ferns, etc.

If you are set on having a particular plant in your house but find that it requires a lot of sun, then you can place it on a windowsill or in a space that gets a lot of natural sunlight. There are lots of ways you can make your indoor garden work for you. All you need is some creativity and understanding of nature.

Nearly any space can become the perfect witch's garden. If you are willing to work towards the end goal you have in mind, then you won't be disappointed with the results. You can always look for inspiration anywhere you go. If you feel inspired to try something new, go ahead and try it. A witch's garden is a personal thing and every choice is yours to make. Don't be afraid to go wild with it.

# HARVESTING, DRYING, AND STORING HERBS

Once you have a garden set up and you're ready to start using your herbs, then you can get on with harvesting, drying, and storing them. There are different ways to go about using your herbs.

You can harvest them in bulk, dry them, and store them so you always have herbs ready for when you need them, or you can just harvest them as you need them. Some recipes and spells in herbal magic require fresh herbs while with others, you can use either fresh or dried herbs.

It's a good idea to learn how to properly harvest, dry, and store your herbs so that you always have them available for quick use but you also encourage continued growth in your garden so your herbs stay fresh and strong.

## Harvesting

You can use whatever tool you want while harvesting your herbs but in tradition an Athame is used. This is a double edged dagger that is usually used in rituals. However, if you're not one for traditions, feel free to use whatever tool you want.

It is better to harvest early in the day before the sun has a chance to rise. Unless you follow a harvest by the moon ritual, any time in the morning before the sun has risen is best. During this time, your garden is covered with early morning dew and the plants have not yet been dried out by the heat of the sun. This is to ensure that the plants maintain their essential oils which are an important ingredient in herbal magic.

## Once-Off Harvesting:

If you need a few fresh herbs for any magical work, then it's important that you only take what you need. You can simply cut off the leaves of stems of the plant that you need. Make sure not to over cut or waste anything.

Some herbs leaves, like basil, are easy to harvest. You can just pinch the stem with your fingers and slid up it. The leaves should be easily stripped off. Other herbs have a woody stem and it's difficult to cut the leaves off by themselves. With these plants you may have to snip the stem off entirely.

When it comes to once-off harvesting flowers, you need to wait until the flowers are in full bloom. Once the flowers are fully developed and opened up then you can snip the heads of the flowers off. Try to take as little of the stems as possible. You just want the bloom and the more of the stems you leave behind the more likely it will grow another flower in its place.

Some forms of herbal magic will ask you to use the seed of a plant. Collecting the seeds is easy, but you can only do so if the seeds are fully developed. This means, in some cases, that the seeds have dried out and are turning brown on their own. The best and easiest way to harvest seeds is with a paper bag. Gently tie a paper bag around the head of the plant whose seeds you want to harvest. Now, shake the plant carefully so that you encourage any dry seeds to fall out of the plant and into the bag. All the fully developed seeds should fall into the bag but if the seeds are not yet developed then they will stay stuck to the plant.

## Bulk Harvesting

Bulk harvesting is usually done when you want to dry and store herbs for later use. This needs to be done carefully. You want to harvest as much as possible so you can dry a huge amount of herbs at once. However, you don't want to harvest so much that you damage the plant and disrupt its ability to continue growing. Make sure you do this early in the morning so the plants maintain their essential oil.

To cut off a bunch of herbs so you can hang them up to dry, simply cut the stems from where they branch off from the main plant. This will make it easier to hang the herbs but it should also encourage new growth in the plant. This method should work for all plants.

## Drying

There are several options when it comes to drying herbs. There is a slow drying process, which is the safest for the herbs, but takes quite long. Then there is a fast drying process that comes with a risk of burning the herbs but it cuts the drying time down significantly. Your skill and confidence in drying herbs will determine which method you use.

### Slow Drying Method

With this method, you will bunch up the herbs into a large bundle. Normally the bundle consists of 12 or fewer stems. Using more stems could make the process difficult. Once you have about a dozen stems firmly packed together tie a string around the bundle. You want the string to be tight enough that the bundle doesn't come undone but try not to damage the herbs in the process. Once the bundle is securely tied together you can hang the herbs in a dry and airy place.

Keep the bundles out of direct sunlight. It might not seem that hot, but the direct sunlight could end up burning the herbs if you're not careful. There can't be too much humidity around the herbs otherwise they won't dry. Hang them on a drying rack in a warm place in your home, out of direct sunlight and surrounded by dry air, and leave them there for about three weeks. To know if the herbs are dry, just pinch one of the leaves with your fingers. If the leaf cracks, then the herbs are fully dry.

If you're using this drying method on plants where you require their seeds or the flowers then use a paper bag. Go through the same method of tying the stems together and hanging them up but tie a paper bag around the head of the plant. While the plant is drying, the seeds and flowers will naturally fall off into the paper bag.

### **Fast Drying Method**

There are two different versions of this method. One version uses an oven, while the other uses a dehydrator if you have one. This is if you're in a hurry and you've run out of a certain herb that you need.

To start you need a baking tray, like the type you bake cookies, and some non-stick paper. You don't want to put any kind of oil or spray on the tray because that will transfer over to the herbs and taint them. Lay the herbs on the tray next to each other and not on top of each other. Put your oven on a low heat and slid the tray in. The low heat will take longer than a higher heat but it will decrease the risk of burning the herbs.

Check the oven continuously to make sure you don't burn the herbs. This method is nice because it fills your house with a lovely smell and the herbs should be ready in about 30 minutes. Be cautious though, everyone's oven has different settings so even on a low temperature the herbs may dry faster than you expect. Keep checking them, remember that if the leaves break when you pinch them, they are ready.

If you're using a dehydrator, the method is basically the same. A dehydrator has a lower temperature setting than an oven so it's safer to use. There is less risk in burning the herbs but it still cuts down on the time it takes to dry them. Check them as much as you can to be safe. Test the leaves to see if they crack or crumble to know when they are ready.

# Storing

Storing your dry herbs can be a fun activity. It's something that allows for creativity and imagination. Dry herbs need to be kept in a cool dry place, away from moisture, heat, or humidity. That is the only rule. Other than that, you can do whatever you want with them.

You should try keeping them in colored glass or ceramic jars to protect them from direct light. However, if you want to put them in clear glass jars, just make sure to keep them in a dark area.

You can maybe decorate the jars to make them seem witchy and look nice. Labeling the jars so you know can identify the herb is a must have. However, you can get creative with this as well by using the herbs witchy or scientific name. As long as you know what herb it is, use whatever name you want for it. If an herb is toxic, you should add that to its label just to be safe.

As for finding a place to store your herbs, get a little creative with that too. Don't keep them above your stove or any place where the temperature might change suddenly. Some Wiccans like to have their own witch's cupboard. It's a cupboard solely dedicated to their herbs. You can store the herbs in the cupboard and even put up a sign and lock it with a chain to add that extra witchy feel.

If you want to keep your herbs out in the open, feel free to do so. Remember to keep certain safety rules in mind. Keep them out of the reach of children or animals. Keep them in a cool, dark place. As long as you keep all of those rules in mind then you can do whatever you want with your herbs.

# A WICCAN'S TOOLS

Everyone has their own toolbox and it is filled with must have tools of the trade. It's the same with Wiccans. There are a few tools you must have if you are choosing to follow the Wiccan path. This list will focus on the tools you will need if you plan on performing any herbal magic. These tools can also be used for other purposes but for now you'll learn how best to use them for your herbal spells, rituals, and magical work.

### 1. An Athame

This is mainly a ritual tool, but it has a huge role to play in herbal magic. An Athame is basically a double edged dagger. You can buy one or make one yourself. It is used in herbal magic for directing energy and harvesting herbs. An Athame is often used to direct energy into objects that are going to be used in spells and rituals but you will mostly be using it to harvest or cut your herbs.

You can use any gardening tool to harvest your herbs, however an Athame is used in most traditions. You should cleanse it each time before using it and focus on directing your energy into the herbs while you are using the Athame.

The best way to direct your energy into the herbs while using the Athame is to visualize it. This is the easiest directing energy method, especially if you are a beginner. Visualize a light pulsing around your body, this is your energy. Picture the light moving around your body, over the Athame, and into the herb you are working with.

### 2. A Cauldron

This is a must have for any magic but it is especially used in herbal magic. Some herbal spells will require you to cook the herbs and this is what you use the cauldron for. A cauldron is better than a normal pot because it is a traditional tool that you can use both indoors and outdoors, depending on your preference.

You should consider having two separate cauldrons just for safety reasons. Some of your spells will require you to use toxic herbs, while other spells may consist of something you can eat or drink. You don't want to make them both in the same cauldron. Even if you clean the cauldron, there is still a risk that the toxic herb will still contaminate your other herbs. It's better to have two cauldrons and separate both toxic and edible herbs.

Make sure to properly clean the cauldrons after and before every use.

### 3. A Staff or A Wand

It may sound a little weird but a wand or staff does have practical uses. I'm not suggesting you point your wand at something, whisper an incantation, and make the object float around. Wands and staffs have a very important use in Wicca, a use they share with an Athame.

A wand or staff is used as a directing tool. You use it to direct your personal energy in a specific direction or into a certain object. Some are able to direct their energy without the help of a wand, staff, or Athame. However, if you are a beginner, it is better to get some kind of directing tool until you have learned the art of directing properly.

Whether you choose a wand or a staff is up to you. Most believe that wands are more feminine while staffs are masculine. In some covens, the male followers carry staffs while the female followers possess wands. However, the choice is still yours based on what you prefer.

### 4. A Robe

Many of those who practice Wicca prefer to perform any spells, rituals, or magical works while dressed in a special robe. The robe is usually white, should cover you from head to toe, and you use a rope to tie around your waste. A robe is not an important tool, but it is a way to ensure that no unwanted energy enters your magical works.

We carry energy within us and there is energy all around us. If you go out into the world dressed in your usual clothes, those clothes will gather up all sorts of energy. You can't be certain that you haven't gathered negative or harmful energy along the way. This is why most Wiccans prefer to cleanse themselves before performing any magic.

The robe is an extra step to take. Instead of performing magic in clothes that could contain harmful energy you put on a cleansed and natural robe. The robe is cleansed before and after it is used and it does not contain any energy other than the energy you put into it. Therefore it cannot bring any unwanted energy into your magical work.

### 5. Candles and Crystals

These tools usually take part in their own category of magic. You get candle magic and you get crystal magic. However, both of them do still play a role in herbal magic. Some herbal spells and recipes will ask you to use a crystal or a candle, so it's best to have a few of them on hand just in case. You don't need to go into too much detail such as size or color but try and get as a variety just so you know you're prepared.

### 6. A Pentacle

This object is only necessary if you follow a certain tradition. In most Wiccan traditions, a pentacle is kept on the altar and is used as a protective talisman in many rituals and it is also used to represent the elements. Another use is to hold objects and tools on the altar and keep them cleansed until they are used in magical works.

A pentacle is a flat, circular piece of material, traditionally wood but metal, clay, and other materials can be used. Magical symbols are then carved into the surface of the material. A symbol can be carved, although a five pointed star (pentagram) is most commonly used.

The pentagram represents the elements which is why the pentacle is usually used in magical ceremonies or placed at the altar. The four bottom points of the star each represent one of the four classical elements. The fifth point of the star, the top point, represents the fifth element the Spirit which is seen in all the other elements.

A pentacle can be bought or you can make one yourself. Making one yourself may be the best option because then you are free to carve any symbol you deem magical onto it.

### 7. A Book of Shadows

Last but probably most important, you will need a book of shadows. A Wiccan's book of shadows acts as many things. It is basically a collection of that Wiccan's knowledge. Wiccans can use their book of shadows as a journal, a recipe book, a spell book, or all three. A Wiccan can take their book of shadows and write down anything they want.

You may have heard about a book of shadows. Some are led to believe that there is only one book of shadows and that is the original one written by Gerald Gardner, but this is false. Anyone can have their personal book of shadows or they can share one with a group of witches or their coven.

When you think of a book of shadows you might picture a giant leather bound book with yellow stained pages, filled with pictures and weird text. That's the kind of stuff you see in the movies. You can have that if that is what you want but if you're looking for something simpler, your book of shadows can be a simple notebook.

In these modern times most Wiccans go as simple as having a digital book of shadows on their computer, laptop, or phone. In the end, your book of shadows is just as personal as your altar or your choice of magical work.

# CHAPTER IV

# A LIST OF MAGICAL HERBS

# HERBS LISTED BY NAME

Here is a complete list of magical herbs alongside the magical properties they are associated with. Some herbs include details about what kind of spells they are mostly used with. This list does not contain all of the herbs used in Wicca but only the most common and powerful herbs.

### Alfalfa (Medicago sativa):
This herb is associated with money, good fortune, cleansing, and healing. It is mostly used in money magic.

### Angelica (Angelica archangelica L.):
This herb is associated with banishing evil, warding off negative energy, protection, and strength. It is commonly used in spells for protection.

### Ash (Fraxinus):
This herb is associated with protection, health, prosperity, and dreams. It is often used in spells for protection and prosperity, but also used in rituals for the sea.

### Astragalus (Astragalus propinquus):
This herb is associated with protection (shielding), health, energy, concentration and mental clarity. It is mostly used in spells for casting a shield, concentration, and clarity.

### Adam and Eve Root (Aplectrum hyemale):
These herbs are mostly associated with love and

happiness and are often used in various love spells.

### African violet (Saintpaulia):
This herb is associated with being spiritual and overall protection. It is mostly only used in spells for protection.

### Allspice (Pimenta dioica):
This herb is associated with strength, perseverance, energy, vitality, harmony, friendly interactions and communication, sympathy, and determination. It is often used in spells to strengthen willpower and energy. It is also used as incense in social gatherings to bring harmony and friendly interactions to the room.

### Adder's tongue (Ophioglossum):
This herb is mostly associated with good health and is used in various healing and good health spells.

### Aloe (Aloe vera):
This herb is associated with persistence, patience, inner health, and resolve. It is mostly used in magic for inner health and healing and is kept in the home to promote healthy living and peace.

### Ague Root (Trichanthera):
This herb is associated with protection and is used in various spells and magic for protection.

### Almond (Prunus dulcis):
This herb is associated with money, good work ethic, and alertness. It is mostly used in money magic to attract money and to promote wealth.

### Alyssum (Lobularia maritima):
This herb is associated with protection, and reducing and moderating anger. The only spells it is used for are protection spells and spells to ward off negative energy.

### Amber (Amber):

This herb is associated with mental focus, mental clarity, and protection. It is mostly used in spells to protect from harm, negative energy, psychic attack, or outside influences.

### Apple and Apple Blossoms (Malus domestica):
These are associated with love, happiness, healing, peace of mind, immortality, success, and contentment. Apples and apple blossoms are often used in spells for love and happiness.

### Avocado (Persea americana):
This is associated with love, beauty, and lust. It is mostly used in love and lust spells but it is also used to promote beauty and health.

### Basil (Ocimum basilicum):
This herb is associated with money, promoting wealthy, prosperity, luck, love, happiness, and peace. Basil is an herb that is most associated with money and wealth. It is said to resemble paper money as it is often used in spells for money and luck. People keep a potted plant of basil in their home or place of work to bring in money and promote luck among other things.

### Bay Leaf (Laurus nobilis):
This herb is associated with protection, good fortune, success and victory, and purification. It is often used in spells for repelling negative energy and for protection.

### Birch Bark (Betula):
This is associated with psychic protection, new beginnings, and strength. It's mostly used in spells for

protection and strength.

### Bay (Laurus nobilis):
This herb is often associated with protection, healing, strength, and purification. It's mostly used for cleansing, purification, healing blessings, and protection spells.

### Blue Sage (Salvia azurea):
This herb is associated with meditation, peace, wisdom, and relaxation. It is mostly used in smudging rituals.

### Cardamom (Elettaria cardamomum):
This herb is associated with love. His properties were also known in the past. The ancient Arabs in fact thought that cardamom had aphrodisiac powers.

### Chamomile (Matricaria chamomilla):
This herb is associated with inner peace, tranquility, sleep, and meditation. It is commonly used in herbal tea magic to promote peaceful sleep and deep meditation.

### Chives (Allium schoenoprasum):
This herb is mostly associated with protection and is used in various protection spells.

### Cinnamon (Cinnamomum verum):
This herb is associated with prosperity, luck, tranquility, protection, strength, and calmness. Cinnamon is known to strengthen the quality of other herbs magical abilities so it's mostly added to other mixtures to strengthen their power.

### Cloves (Syzygium aromaticum):
This herb is associated with protection, warding off negative energy, psychic shielding, courage, self-confidence, and love. It is rarely used in anything else besides various protection spells.

### Cedar (Cedrus):
This herb is associated with confidence, strength, protection, purification, healing, and powerful energy. It's mostly used in magic for protection, blessings for health, and purification.

### Cherry and Cherry Blossom (Prunus avium):
This herb is associated with love, joy, happiness, and good feelings. Both the cherries and the blossoms are used to promote joy, happiness, and love in your life.

### Club moss (Lycopodiopsida):
This herb is associated with protection and powerful energy. Let it grow around your house for powerful protection.

### Comfrey (Symphytum):
This is often associated with safety and money but it's usually only used in money magic.

### Coriander (Coriandrum sativum):
This herb is associated with love, happiness, healing, good health, and protection. It's used in spells for love, healing, and protection.

### Cumin (Cuminum cyminum):
This herb is associated with tranquility, peace, and health. It's mostly used to promote peace and tranquility.

### Caraway (Carum carvi):
This herb is associated with good fortune, luck,

prosperity, passion, and sensuality. It's often used in magic for good fortune and luck but it's also used in love and lust spells.

### Cayenne (Capsicum frutescens):
This herb is associated with purification, cleansing, protection, and warding of negativity. It is often added to other herbal mixtures to strengthen and speed up their effects.

### Daisy (Bellis perennis):
This herb is associated with lust and love and is used in many different spells and teas to promote love and lust.

### Dandelion (Taraxacum):
This is a very spiritual herb and is mostly associated with making wishes, divination, calling spirits, and dreaming. It's mostly used in wishing spells, and divination.

### Dill (Anethum graveolens):
This herb is associated with focus, concentration, mental strength and agility. It is often used in spells and blessings for health.

### Daffodil (Narcissus):
This herb is often associated with love, fertility, good fortune and luck. It is mostly used for love and fertility spells.

### Elder (Sambucus):

This is a very powerful tree and every part of it is used in all forms of magic. Elderberries are associated with connection between the physical and spiritual realm. The wood from the Elder is associated with healing, protection, sleep, prosperity, and warding off evil.

You can make a wand out of Elder wood to bring protection magic into your work and summon spirits easily. In other spells and blessings you can use the oil from the flowers of an Elder or just use the flowers and leaves. It's often used for blessings of health and protection.

### Elm (Ulmus):

The Elm is associated with everything to do with love and it is used in various love spells. Just having an Elm nearby your home attracts and encourages love.

### Eucalyptus (Eucalyptus globulus):

This herb is associated with healing, spiritual cleansing, and purification. It is often used in spells for health and used in rituals for cleansing.

### Fern (Leptosporangiate fern):
This herb is associated with dispelling negative energy, purification, and cleansing. It is often used in rituals to cleanse and purify, but it is also kept in a pot around the house to ward of negative and harmful energy.

### Fennel (Foeniculum vulgare):
This herb is commonly associated with protection, strength, and healing. It's mostly used in magic for protection and strength.

### Figwort (Scrophularia):
This plant is associated with health and protection, and is mostly used in blessing for health and protection.

### Foxglove (Digitalis):
This herb is associated with protection and is used in various spells for protection from any negative, harmful, and unwanted energy.

### Frankincense (Boswellia sacra):
This herb is associated with meditation and spiritual awareness. It's mostly used for blessings and it aids meditation.

### Frangipani (Plumeria):
This herb is associated with admiration, trust, love, happiness, and open relationships. It is often used for love, happiness, and general relationship spells.

### Garlic (Allium sativum):

This herb is mostly associated with cleansing, purification, warding off negative and harmful energy, thoughts, and feelings. It's also connected to prosperity, money, and protection. In movies they use garlic to ward off vampires and people see it as a silly joke. However, garlic is used as protection against not only outside harm but also harm from within. It wards of negative energy, depression, and harmful thoughts.

It's also used in magic to attract money.

### Ginger (Zingiber officinale):

This herb is powerful and potent. It is associated with confidence, adventure, sexuality, prosperity, and sensuality. It's usually added to other herbal mixtures to strength their magical attributes as long as their correspondents are similar.

### Hazel (Corylus):

This herb is associated with luck, making wishes, protection, and fertility. It is often used in blessings for protection. You can have hazel near your home to promote luck and you can use the leaves to make wishes.

### Holly (Ilex):

This is used for luck,

protection, and dream magic. Having a holly near your home will promote protection and luck in your life. Otherwise, it is used in dream sachets and other dream magic.

### Hyssop (Hyssopus officinalis):
This herb is associated with cleansing and purification. It's mostly used before rituals or any magical work to bless and cleanse your altar and everything in the area.

### Hibiscus (Hibiscus rosa-sinensis):
This herb is mostly associated with love and lust, and is sometimes used for divination. Most of the spells its used for are for love.

### Honeysuckle (Lonicera periclymenum):
This herb is associated with affection, love, and fidelity. It's often used to make love charms, in which the wearer dreams of their true love.

### Ivy (Hedera):
This herb is associated with healing and protection. It's often used in healthy blessings and protection spells.

### Irish moss (Chondrus crispus):
This is associated with money, protection, and luck. You can grow it around your house and inside your garden to attract money, luck, and protect your home.

### Jasmine (Jasminum):
This herb is associated with love, lust, spiritual aid, success, and it has a strong connection to the moon. It's used in lunar magic for love and spiritual awakening.

### Knotweed (Fallopia japonica):
This herb is associated with health and is used in blessings and spells for health.

### Lemon (Citrus Limon):
This plant is associated with purification, cleansing, and spiritual opening. It's mostly used in blessings for purification and cleansing before rituals.

### Lavender (Lavandula):
This herb is associated with love, peace, protection, tranquility, and good sleep. It's mostly used in spells for love. Plant it around the house to promote peace and tranquility, and added protection.

### Lilac (Syringa vulgaris):
This herb has been associated with protection and warding off evil for a very long time. In New England, lilacs were planted are the house or in an area to protect it

from evil. You can plant lilac around your home or even keep it inside your home to protect you from negative and harmful energy. The fresh flowers can also be used in rituals and blessings.

### Lily (Lilium):
This plant is commonly associated with love and protection but it is mostly used to break love spells.

### Lime (Citrus aurantifolia):
This herb is associated with strength, protection, purification, tranquility, and peace. It's mostly used in spells to strengthen love.

### Leek (Allium porrum):
This herb is associated with love, protection, warding off negative and harmful energy. It's mostly used in spells for protection and warding off negative or harmful energy.

### Luminous Moss (Schistostega pennata)
This is associated with money, good fortune, and luck. Allowing moss to grow near your home or work place will attract money and good fortune.

### Mint (Mentha):
This herb is associated with money, prosperity, wealth, energy and vitality. It's often used in spells to attract prosperity and wealth.

### Mandrake (Mandragora Officinarum):
This herb comes in two forms. One is a long root that resembles a carrot and it

is associated with money, fertility, love, sex, good luck, and virility. It's often cut up into small pieces when it's used in magic. The other form of the mandrake is shaped like a man with two arms, two legs, and a head. This is a very rare form of the mandrake plant. This form is never cut up and is used in magic whole. It's often used in powerful magic to attract spirits or familiars. The whole mandrake acts as a vessel for the spirit of familiar as long as it is cleansed before use and fed with milk or wine regularly.

Mandrake is poisonous. It should be handled with care, kept away from pregnant women, and you must avoid ingesting it.

### Mistletoe (Viscum album):
This herb is associated with prosperity, money, business, love, and happiness. Mistletoe is often used to attract wealth and promote prosperity but it's also used in a few love spells.

Mistletoe is a toxic herb. It should be handled with care, kept away from pregnant women, and you should avoid ingesting it.

### Meadowsweet (Filipendula ulmaria):
This herb is associated with love, happiness, peace, tranquility, and divination. It's mostly used in blessings and spells for love, happiness, and peace.

### Moonwort (Botrychium lunaria):
This herb is associated with love, happiness, and money. It's used mostly in spells to attract money, promote wealth, and to find love.

### Mugwort (Artemisia vulgaris):
This herb is mostly associated with strengthening psychic ability, divination, dreaming and scrying. It is often used in moon magic and lucid dreaming magic.

### Nutmeg (Myristica fragrans):

This herb is associated with clarity, emotional openness, perception, confidence, and social interaction. It's mostly used to aid clarity and perception. You can also burn some nutmeg incense to fill the room during social interactions. This will promote good feelings in the room and self-confidence.

### Nettle (Urtica dioica):

This herb is associated with protection, courage, healing, warding off negative energy, and deterring evil. It's mostly used in spells and blessings for protection. You can hang it around your house and grow it outside your home to ward of negative and harmful energy.

### Oregano (Origanum vulgare):

This herb is associated with joy, vitality, strength, and energy. It's mostly used in magic to promote happiness, vitality, and good energy.

### Orange and Orange Blossom (Citrus):

These are associated with harmony, tranquility, peace, love, emotional openness, prosperity, purification, and stability. This herb is connected to the sun so doing magic in the sunlight produces powerful results. It's used mostly for love, peace, happiness, and harmony spells.

### Orchid (Orchidaceae):
This herb is associated with strengthening will power and memory, focus, and concentration. Keep this plant in your home to promote good memory and strong will power.

### Oak (Quercus):
This herb is associated with protection and strength. It is a plant that is closely associated with the horned god. Having it in your garden will protect you and your home from all negative or harmful energy.

### Parsley (Petroselinum crispum):
This herb is associated with lust, protection, warding off negative energy, and purification. It's mostly used in protection and lust spells.

### Peppermint (Mentha balsamea):
This herb is mostly associated with protection. Plant it outside your doors and windows to protect you home and carry it with you as a shield.

### Pennyroyal (Mentha pulegium):
This herb is associated with protection, peace, tranquility, and strength. It's mostly used in protection spells. Carry it around with you to promote peace and tranquility in your life.

### Pansy (Viola tricolor subsp. hortensis):
This herb is associated with promoting feelings of love, love divination, and it is used in rain magic.

### Poppy (Papaver somniferum):
This herb is associated with fertility, money, good fortune, luck, and love. It is often used in magic for money, luck, and love.

### Patchouli (Pogostemon cablin):
This herb is associated with love, attraction, fertility, and sexuality. It's mostly used in spells for love and sex.

### Primrose (Primula vulgaris):
This herb is often associated with love and protection but it's mostly used for love magic.

### Rose (Rosaceae):
Roses are associated with love, healing, luck, protection, love, divination, and protection. The different colors of the roses are associated with their own magical abilities. Roses are often used to make love charms.

### Rosemary (Rosmarinus officinalis):
This herb is associated with love, lust, protection, purification, mental energy, healing, youthful energy, and sleep. It's mostly used in spells for love and lust but it is also used in protection and health blessings.

### Ragwort (Jacobaea vulgaris):
This herb is associated with various forms of protection, and is used in various protection spells and blessings.

### Rue (Primula vulgaris):
This herb is associated with mental strength, love, health, healing, and warding off negative and harmful energy. It's mostly used in protection and health blessings and spells.

### Sage (Salvia officinalis):
This herb is associated with cleansing, protection, purification, promoting wisdom, and clarity. It's often used in smudging for cleansing and protection spells, and herbal bundles.

### Saffron (Crocus sativus):
This herb is associated for promoting clarity, prosperity, wealth, and good fortune. It is often used to attract wealth and fortune.

### Sunflower (Helianthus):
This herb is associated with health, making wishes, fertility, and wisdom. It's mostly used in wishing spells and healthy blessings.

### Sow Thistle (Sonchus):
This herb is associated with strength, protection, and repelling evil. It's usually used in protection spells but just planting it outside or inside your home should keep you protected.

### Sweet pea (Lathyrus odoratus):

This herb is associated with loyalty, friendship, affection, and companionship. It is used in magic to attract loyalty, new friends, and companions.

### Spiderwort (Tradescantia):
This is one of the few herbs used for love magic that is especially powerful.

### Spanish moss (Tillandsia usneoides):
This herb is mostly associated with protection, warding off negative energy, and dispelling negativity. Allow this to grow around your home and in your garden to protect your household.

### Spearmint (Mentha spicata):
This herb is associated with protection, repelling negative energy, strengthens mental clarity, and focus. Spearmint is mostly added to other herbal mixtures to improve the strength of their magical qualities.

### Star Anise (Illicium verum):
This herb associated with good fortune, luck, clarity, and psychic dreams. It is often used to make charms for good luck and safe travels.

### Thyme (Thymus vulgaris):
This herb is associated with healing, purification, strength, loyalty, and affection. It's mostly used in healing spells and used to attract loyalty and affection from others.

### Tuberose (Polianthes tuberosa):
This herb is associated with

peace, serenity, tranquility, love, and lust. It is often used in spells to attract love and promote a peaceful life.

### **Vanilla (Vanilla planifolia):**
This herb is associated with joy, happiness, good fortune, and friendship. It's mostly used to promote joy and happiness in life.

### **Violet (Viola):**
This herb is associated with happiness, peace, tranquility, dreams, and stimulates creativity. It's mostly used for dream magic.

### **Vervain (Verbena):**
This herb is associated with peace, tranquility, protection, warding off negative energy, money, and purification. Vervain is brewed into tea to ward off negative or harmful energy. The leaves can be burnt to attract wealth. It can be added to water and placed on the altar for cleansing and purification. It can also be added to dill to banish harmful energy. Vervain is often added to other herbal mixtures to strengthen their magical qualities.

### **Valerian (Valeriana officinalis):**
This herb is associated with protection and warding off negative and harmful energy. It's used in many different forms of protection and shielding magic.

### **Vetivert (Chrysopogon zizanioides):**
This herb is associated with protection, warding off negativity, money, wealth, and prosperity. It is mostly used in spells to attract money and repel negative energy.

### Witch Hazel (Hamamelis):

This herb is associated with healing, protection, wisdom, comfort, and soothing anger. It is mostly used in health blessings and protection spells.

### Wormwood (Artemisia absinthium):

This herb is a more hateful and negative herb. It's associated with hexes and curses. However it can also be used for psychic vision and invoking spirits. Wormwood is used to cast curses and hexes but can sometimes be used in reverse magic to reverse those hexes and curses.

### White Sage (Salvia apiana):

This herb is associated with healing, cleansing, meditation, and blessings. It's mostly used in health blessings and for cleansing purposes.

### Willow (Salix):

This herb is associated with love, healing, and happiness. It's often used in spells to strengthen love and overcome sadness. It's also used in some moon magic.

### Wintergreen (Gaultheria procumbens):

This herb is associated with health, tranquility and peace. It's often used in spells to repel negative energy and disease.

Wintergreen is a very toxic herb. Handle with care, keep it away from pregnant women, children, and pets. Do not ingest.

### Wood Aloe (Aloidendron barberae):

This herb is associated with prosperity, wealth, protection, and success. It's mostly used in spells for protection and wealth.

### Yarrow (Achillea millefolium):

This herb is associated with protection, confidence, courage, and love. It's mostly used in spells to attract love, promote courage and confidence, and in protection spells.

You may not want to look through a whole list of herbs to find the one you need for what you want. If you want to make a love spell and you just need to know which herbs are used for that, without having to go through a bunch of other herbs to do so, then you can refer to the next list. This list will contain all of the useful herbs in Wicca based on their attributes.

## Toxic Herbs

Toxic and poisonous herbs are often used in herbal magic. If you follow all the right safety precautions and you know how to use the herbs then they aren't dangerous to use. It's important to know what herbs pose a danger to your or anyone else's health. It's also important to properly label all harmful herbs so not only you know of their danger but others can know as well.

The best way to avoid endangering yourself or others is by avoiding any of the toxic herbs you are aware of. It's understandable if you want to work with these herbs. Practicing herbal magic means using all of the herbs that nature has made available to you. Even if the herbs you need to use can harm you it's still an appealing part of the process.

If you are planning on using any dangerous herbs then read through this part of the book carefully. Keep this information on you whenever you're working with herbs. And, of course, be cautious.

## Dangerous Herbs for Pets

- **Holly berries** can be dangerous for both dogs and cats if ingested.
- **Mistletoe berries** are poisonous towards both cats and dogs and can lead to death if an excessive amount is ingested.
- **Pennyroyal oil** is extremely harmful to cats, especially pregnant cats. It's probably safe to keep it away from both dogs and cats.
- **Foxglove** can kill dogs and cats if it is ingested.
- **Jimson weed** is harmful not only to cats and dogs but can also harm large animals, such as horses.
- **Buckeye** can be extremely dangerous to both dogs and cats. Ingesting an excessive amount can even lead to seizures.
- **Chamomile** is slightly dangerous to both dogs and cats causing vomiting and diarrhea but nothing more serious than that.

Most of us have some household pets and we all love

them. So if you have a love for herbal magic but want to keep your pets safe, it is recommended that you keep these herbs far away from them. Take extra precaution and make sure that your pets are out of the house or at least out of the room when you are using these herbs.

## Dangerous Herbs for Pregnant Woman:

- **Yarrow** can cause menstruation in pregnant woman.
- **Comfrey** can cause both the woman and the fetus to have liver damage.
- **Basil** can cause menstruation in pregnant woman.
- **Angelica** can cause early contractions in pregnant women.
- **Catnip**, although great for cats, can cause early contractions and it acts as a uterine stimulant.
- **Mugwort** can not only cause menstruation but can also cause birth defects in the fetus.
- **Rosemary** can also cause early contractions.
- **Pennyroyal** is a uterine stimulate and can cause early contractions.
- **Feverfew** can cause menstruation and cause birth defects.
- **Black cohosh** can cause a miscarriage.
- **Goldenseal** can cause a miscarriage.
- **Mistletoe** can cause a miscarriage.

You need to take extra care if you are pregnant or if you are around someone who is pregnant. For the safety of the mother and the baby these herbs should be avoided completely. Most of the time the harmful part comes from ingesting the herb but sometimes just inhaling the scent of the herbs can be harmful. It's safer to avoid all of these herbs, especially the last three, at all costs.

Ultimately, your safety and that of everyone else should always be your first and last thought. As a last precaution you should just avoid any herbs you don't know or are unsure of.

For more information check **Appendix I**, you'll find herbs listed by their attributes.

# CHAPTER V

# HOW TO USE HERBS

One of the most alluring attributes of herbal magic is how versatile it is. There are so many different uses for so many different herbs. There are hundreds of useful herbs and a variety of ways to use them. This is what makes herbal magic one of the greatest parts of the Wiccan lifestyle. The fact that Wicca is a nature centered religion isn't the only reason most Wiccans prefer practicing the art of nature.

For centuries, nature has been used for medicine as well as beauty products. Many plants were believed to have sacred powers of protection and strength long before Wicca was a widely recognized religion. Even before Wicca existed, nature was worshipped and used by many different cultures.

If you wish to dive deep into all the benefits and uses of herbs then read on.

# WICCAN USES FOR HERBS

Herbs are used and blended together in many different forms. A witch wanting to master all forms of herbal magic need only apply themselves to the wonder of nature. Just like we are able to adapt and change to different situations, so can nature. In herbal magic we simply take advantage of the versatile nature of herbs.

I'll walk you through all the different herbal methods.

**Incense** – With this method, herbs whose magical properties correspond with your current desire are burnt.

**Oils** – In this method, an herb or a mixture of herbs is blended with oil to create its own herbal oil. There are many different types of oils and many different ways to use the oil.

**Teas** – There are different kinds of teas that are made in herbal magic. One of the types you can drink and the other is known as a wash.

**Bundles** – This is a bundle of herbs with certain magical abilities that are hung as magical decoration.

**Baths** – This is one of the best and most relaxing methods of herbal magic, especially for beginners.

These are only a few methods of herbal magic. The most important thing about herbal magic is to remember that it may not be easy, but it is rewarding. All of this will probably seem overwhelming for a beginner. Even if you've never made your own herbal oil before or you don't know how to make tea with herbs you don't have to worry. This is yet another wonderful part about herbal magic. If you're completely new to it, don't stress, you can learn fairly easy. The things that seem mysterious to you won't be so for much longer.

## Magical Oils

Herbal oils are made from all different parts of an herb. They are distilled from leaves, roots, flower petals, seeds, and bark of any useful plant. Although you can buy already prepared magical oils making your own tends to be less expensive. Also making your own oil has the same benefits as growing your own garden in a sense.

All you need are the herbs with magical properties that you desire and carrier oil. Carrier oil is premade oil you use to dilute the magical oils you've made. This makes them safer for use. Commonly used carrier oils are almond oil, olive oil, safflower oil, and grape seed oil.

There are two different methods when it comes to making magical oils. Both methods are simple and can be used with any and all herbs.

### Hot Oil Method

This is the fastest method to use in case you urgently need some magical oils. For this, you can use both fresh and dried herbs. If you're using fresh herbs, you'll need to use twice as much than if you are using dry herbs.

So for instance, take 250 grams of dry herbs/500 grams of fresh herbs, and combine that with about 750 milliliters of either vegetable oil or olive oil. Put this in your cauldron and gently heat the mixture over your stove. It should take about three hours for the mixture to be boiled properly. Once the herbs have infused with the oil you can take a piece of cheesecloth or a similar material and drain the oil from the herbs.

The herbs have infused with the oil so right now all you want is the oil. Take the remainder of the herbs and bury it in your garden. You can throw the herbs away but if you put it back into your garden it can feed your plants and you're giving back to nature for what it has given to you.

Once the oil is separated from the herbs, you can put it in a dark, airtight bottle. You need the bottle to be dark so it keeps out the sun and you need the lid to be air tight so no oil can leak out. Label the bottle and store it in a cool dry place.

### **Cold Oil Method**

For this, you can use both dried and fresh herbs but the process is better with fresh herbs. This method takes longer, but it will yield more powerful oil.

Take a big jar and fill it with the herb or herbs that you want to use. Then gently pour some olive oil or vegetable oil over the herbs until the jar is full. Close the lid tightly. Make sure the jar is airtight to avoid any leakage. Leave the jar on a windowsill where it will be exposed to the sun for about two or three weeks.

After the two or three weeks have passed, drain the oil through cheesecloth or similar material and then place it back into the jar with some fresh herbs. Place it back on the windowsill for further two or three weeks. When you drain the oil again, it will be ready.

This method is nice because even though it takes longer, it's easier to make a big batch.

No matter which method you use, you can make the oil as simple or complex as you want. You can make magical oil with one type of herb or you can blend different herbs with similar properties together. The more herbs you add to the mixture, the more complex it is to make, but you will also make a more powerful and magical oil.

For many Wiccans magical oils are a must have. They are used for all sorts of things from rituals, cleansing, and spells. However, unlike most other herbs and ingredients in magical work, magical oils tend to be more of a side character than the center of the show. Most of the time when magical oils are used it is alongside something else and not normally alone.

Magical oils are used to anoint and cleanse rituals tools and often even the body before a ritual or spell casting. Oils are also used in other forms of magic, from candle magic to crystal magic and more.

As usual, the magical property of an herb is how you determine what you use the oil for. If you want to use the oil to cleanse or purify anything then you need to use herbs that are associated with cleansing and purification. Oils can be used for almost anything. You can even add them to baths and moisturizers for beauty magic.

### Safety Tips For Magical Oils
1. Keep magical oils out of reach from children and away from pets.
2. Make sure your magical oils are always sealed and packed away properly.
3. Don't consume, ingest or use undiluted oils. Always dilute oils with carrier oil before use.
4. Make sure you know what herbs are toxic and what herbs are safe before making or using any oil.
5. Do not use undiluted or toxic oil for cooking purposes. Only use diluted oil that is made from food safe herbs.
6. Keep oil out of your eyes and away from your

nose, ears, and mouth.
7. If you're pregnant, try to avoid the use of any oils.
8. Test any oils on a small part of your skin before using it properly. If you see any redness, feel itchiness or irritations on your skin then don't use the oil further.
9. Always consult with a doctor before using any herbal oils you are unsure of.

**Using Magical Oils**
There are many different ways to use magical oils.

## *Beauty*

You can use them for beauty methods. Lavender, rosemary, chamomile, and sandalwood are all soothing herbs with an attractive fragrance. You can add a few drops of oil made from these herbs to your moisturizer and rub it into your skin.

You can add some magical oils to your shampoo and conditioner for a natural, magical hair treatment. Add some rosemary for dark hair and chamomile for light hair.

## *Cooking*

You can add food-safe magical oils to your daily cooking to add some magic to your life. You can bring some extra luck into your life by making some oil with luck, allspice for instance, and adding it to your cooking. You can do the same with prosperity, wealth or anything else you feel is lacking in your life.

You can also make oil with herbs associated with love and cook or bake it into some food for a special someone. Make sure to think of the one you love while making the oil and then while cooking with it. Give the food to the one you love and the magic should start working.

Are you interested in bringing a little magic into your

kitchen? In my book **The Kitchen Witch** you will find lots of recipes and tips to make your every meal special.

## *Anointing*

This is what magical oils are most popular for. Anointing is when you take some oil and rub it on a tool or object to charge it with power. You can use oils to anoint your ritual tools and altar space before performing a ritual or spell casting. You can also use oils to anoint any object before using it in magical works, like anointing a candle with oils before performing a spell with it. You can even anoint your body with oils before a ritual.

These are only some of the ways you can use oil in magic.

For beginners, it might not be easy choosing what kind of magical oil you want to make and work with. As with most things in Wicca, the choice is up to you. It depends on what kind of magic you want to perform and what your end goal is for the oil you're making.

Commonly used oils for beginners are made out of lavender or lemon. Both are extremely fragrant, easy to work with, and inexpensive to make. Some other common oils involve using cinnamon, frankincense, and myrrh. These have been used by herbalists for centuries because of their widespread magical abilities and sweet fragrance. So don't be afraid to experiment and get creative.

## *Simple Money Drawing Oil*

This oil may look complex but it is simple to blend. You need to make the magical oils separately before blending them together.

You need:
- Patchouli oil (4 drops)
- Cypress oil (2 drops)

- Bergamot oil (3 drops)
- Lavender oil (1 drop)

Make these oils separately using either the cold or hot oil method. Then take the required amount of the separate oils and mix them together.

Rub a small bit of this oil into your hands to draw new money to you. You can also take a coin and soak it in oil overnight. The next day take the coin out of the oil and keep it on you to attract money your way.

## Incense and Smudging

Both incense and smudging are similar acts of magic. They involve burning dried herbs in order to release their magical abilities into the universe using their smoke and scent. Even with this in common, incense and smudging are quite different from each other. Incense is usually more complex than smudging bundles as it is made from a mixture of different dried herbs, magical oils, and ever powdered herbs. Smudging bundles are made from a bundle of dried herbs tied together with a string or even a single sprig of dried herbs. Incense is a traditional part of Wicca, whereas smudging is an ancient practice that has been around for centuries.

Incense is used a lot in spell work, but smudging is mostly used beforehand to cleanse or purify an area before any magical work can be done.

### Smudging

A smudge bundle is made up of at least a dozen sprigs of herbs all tied together with some string. You can use a dozen sprigs of the same herb or you can make a mixture of different herbs with the same magical properties. Smudging bundles are traditionally used for cleansing or purification, but with a bit of creativity, you can probably use them for other effects.

With the smudging bundles, you would normally use a

candle or a match to light the end of the herbs. You don't want to set it completely on fire you just want it to start smoking. Then hold the bundle at the far end and walk around the area you wish to cleanse or purify. The smoke is where the magic is. You want the smoke to fill the area and leave its magical mark everywhere.

Smudging bundles can be used multiple times and they last for a while. When you're done using it, you can simply put out the flame and pack the bundle away. The bundles are also easy to work with and hold. However, you don't have to use a full bundle when smudging.

Single smudges use one or two sprigs of herbs. With a single smudge, you light the end of a single sprig of herb and place it on a plate and then carry it on a skillet. This is for safety reasons. Make sure the sprig is at least four inches long for further safety. With single smudges, you only need to wait until the sprig of herb has burned away completely.

### Incense

Incense is a form of art. Incense is made up of plant material. This can be the bark, leaves, seeds, flowers, or roots of any herb. Incense is sometimes blended with magical oils and other ingredients then burnt or smoldered. When it comes to incense, the simplest concoctions are usually the most powerful. One ingredient can give you the results you desire so all you really need to know is the magical properties of herbs and how those properties can benefit the goal you have in mind.

For example, you can burn allspice to attract money and bring luck into your life. You can smolder some sage to promote a healthy life. This is as simple as you can get and the effects show for themselves.

Incense is used for the magical vibrations it lets out into the air while burning. It can be used as a spell itself, in a ritual or blessing, and sometimes it's just burnt in the background during some other magical work.

To burn incense is a bit of an art itself. You need to

ignite a charcoal block and place it in an incense dish or another heat proof container. Some people like to use a bowl filled with sand or salt to add a witchy feel to the process. While the charcoal is burning, you can sprinkle your incense blend over it. Sprinkle a little bit at a time so the scent is not too overpowering. All herbs work better as incense when they've been grounded.

An important thing to remember when working with incense is that sweet smelling herbs don't always smell the same when they're burnt. So don't be surprised if your lavender doesn't smell as nice as you were expecting.

## Simple Prosperity Incense

This is a simple incense blend that will attract wealth to you and your home.

You need:
- Cinnamon (1 part)
- Citron (1 part)
- Nutmeg (1 part)
- Lemon Balm (1 part)
- Frankincense (2 part)

Burn these together and you should see some new wealth in your life.

## Love Smudging Bundle

This is a simple smudging bundle you can make to attract love. You can also use a single smudge by picking anyone of the herbs that are associated with love. Just remember that the more herbs you use, the stronger the magic will be.

You need:
- Lavender (3 sprigs)
- Rosemary (3 sprigs)
- Vanilla (3 sprigs)
- Rose (3 stems, without leaves or thorns)

Tie them all together with a string. While gathering the

herbs and tying them together, try and visualize new love entering your life. Don't think of someone specific as those kinds of love spells usually don't work. Think of the qualities that your ideal partner would have and imagine meeting someone with those qualities. Keep these thoughts in mind as you use the smudging bundle around your home. Do this once a day until the smudging bundle is finished or new love has come into your life.

## Charms, Sachets, and Dream Pillows

Charms, Sachets, and Dream Pillows are similar magical creations but they have different uses. Charms are something we make to carry with us. Sachets are usually something we make to burn, bury or hide somewhere during a spell. Dream Pillows are like sachets but they are made with very specific herbs and placed under our pillows while we sleep. All of these can be simple or complex and they can be made to fit a specific desire or reach a certain goal.

### Charms

A charm is usually a small bag, which is composed of a natural material, and tied closed with a string. The bag is filled with different herbs. The herbs you put in the bag depend on your reasons for making the charm. If you're making the charm for protection reasons, then you would put herbs that have protecting properties in the bag. The color of the bag usually corresponds with the herbs in the bag. If you're making a protective charm, then the color of the bag should correspond with that.

Once the bag is full, you can tie it closed and carry it around with you. You can carry the charm in your pocket or even tie a longer string on it so you can wear the charm as a necklace. Charms are great for protection, luck, and strength spells. You carry them with you and the magic is always there no matter what.

## Sachets

A sachet is like a charm but made for certain spells. Sachets are also made of a bag filled with herbs and tied closed with a string. With sachets, however, the bag is made of a mesh like material. Again, the herbs you put into the sachet and the color of the bag all depend on what your intention is for the sachet.

Sachets are commonly made during spells for love, money, luck, and other similar things. The spell would normally have you burn the sachet or bury it. Sometimes the directions will tell you to hide the sachet somewhere only you know where it is, and only when your goal is reached, do you take the sachet and burn or bury it.

Sometimes sachets are made for baths as well. You throw the sachet into the bath and let the herbs soak into the water. If you're using a sachet for a bath, be cautious that you don't use any toxic or harmful herbs.

## Dream Pillows

These are a more complex creation. It involves making your own tiny pillow to put underneath the pillow you sleep on. You need to take two small rectangular shaped pieces of material. Put them together and sew three sides together, leaving a third side open so you can put the herbs in. Turn the pillow inside out, place the herbs you've chosen, fresh or dried, in the pillow then sew the third side shut. If you aren't willing to sew or if you aren't very good at sewing, you can use a bag with a drawstring or just make a sachet to put underneath your pillow.

There are a few herbs that are used to influence or enhance dreams. Some of these herbs can even make you sleep better if you have problems getting to sleep. To create the right mix of herbs to put into your dream pillow, you need to know what herbs are used for dreams and sleep. You can put herbs directly connected to dreams and sleep and then you can add other herbs to further specify your dreams.

If you want to dream about love, add in an herb that is

connected to love. If the dream pillow makes you dream about this love, you know it will enter your life soon. You can do the same for luck, wealth, friendship, and more.

It's important not to overuse a dream pillow. If the dream pillow has given you the dream you wanted, take the herbs out of the pillow and burn or bury them. If you haven't found your dream yet, keep the dream pillow until you do.

## *Simple Luck Charm*

This is a simple charm that even a beginner can make. This is to bring good luck and fortune your way as long as you carry it with you.

You need:
- Cinnamon (1 stick)
- Dried Chamomile (2 flowers)
- Bay Leaf (1 large leaf)
- Candle (1 with color corresponding with luck)
- A pencil

Place all of the ingredients by your altar and light the candle. Make sure you're thinking about how much luck you want the charm to bring you when you light the candle. You want to put some of your energy into the candle so it can be transferred into the charm.

Place the cinnamon and dried chamomile into your bag. Then use a pencil to write on the bay leaf. You want to write something about luck. You don't need to write anything long, complicated, or specific. You can write something as simple as, "Luck come my way" or "Let my day be filled with luck." Make sure the word "luck" is capitalized. Place the bay leaf into the bag with the other herbs and tie it closed.

Put the charm next to the candle and leave it there for a while so the energy you put into the candle can charge the magic in the charm. Blow out the candle and keep the charm on you at all times to promote luck in your life.

## *Easy Love Sachet*

This is quite easy to make and the spell is simple to perform. It will bring new love into your life.

You need:
- Lavender (1 sprig)
- Rosemary (1 sprig)
- Vanilla Oil (2 drops)
- A pink bag
- A pink candle

Take all the ingredients to your altar and light the candle. When lighting the candle, try visualizing the qualities you want in your ideal partner. Don't be too specific. While keeping the image of your ideal partner in mind, place the lavender and rosemary inside the pink bag. Put the vanilla oil in the bag on top of the herbs and tie the bag up tight.

Get a heatproof, metal dish and place it in front of the candle. Hover the sachet over the candle for a moment and visualize your ideal partner for the last time. Let the sachet catch fire, place it in the heatproof dish, and leave it to burn through.

It might be hard, but for the spell to work quickly, you should try not to think about your ideal partner. If you've done the spell right, trust that the love you seek will find you.

## Magical Teas and Washes

Herbal teas are part of an ancient art. Herbs have been added to boiled water and drunk for medicinal and magical purposes for a long time. Magical teas are a big part of herbal magic. A magical wash is a tea that you can't ingest. Magical teas are made out of food-safe herbs, which are safe to ingest for most people. However, washes are made the same way as a tea, The herbs used in a magical wash are safe for skin contact, but not for ingestion.

## Magical Tea

In ancient times, magical teas were used to heal the body, mind, and soul. Tea was used as a remedy for any physical pain, emotional problems, and even spiritual concerns. Magical teas are probably the most powerful form of herbal magic because the herbs are allowed to directly interact with the body. In most other forms of herbal magic, the herbs don't get any direct contact so some of their power is left unused.

One of the more appealing parts or herbal teas is that they look like a completely normal task. No one will know that you're actually performing some magic. It adds a feeling of excitement and makes you feel as though you are a secret witch hiding from the world around you.

Magical teas are mostly used for medicinal and healing purposes but you can use any herbs you want for any purpose. Of course you have to be mindful of the kind of herbs that are safe to ingest. You can only make herbal teas out of food safe herbs.

## Magical Washes

Herbal washes are prepared the same way as an herbal tea but it is not made for the purpose of ingesting. Washes are used to cleanse the body before rituals or magical work. Washes can also be used for other purposes such as attracting luck and prosperity to your life.

Depending on your goal or intention, you can choose one or more herbs whose magical properties correspond with your goal. Next, boil some water and pour it over the herbs. You don't want the water to be actively boiling or it will be too hot for your skin. Even after you pour it over the herbs you may want to wait until the water has cooled slightly.

Washes are just as versatile as teas and can have many

uses. Although its many uses are usually to cleanse and purify your body.

## *A Simple Divination Tea Recipe*

Dandelion has a strong connection with psychic powers and divination. However, it doesn't have a very nice taste. You may want to add some natural sweeteners like honey.

You need:
- Some boiling water (1 cup)
- Dandelion leaf or root (1 teaspoon)
- Some natural sweetener for taste

Put the dandelion leaf or root in the bottom of the cup and pour the actively boiling water over it. Add the natural sweetener if you want. Sit down in a comfortable place and stir the tea calmly. When it is at a drinkable temperature, slowly sip the tea. Take your time to enjoy the tea and don't rush it. Once the herb enters your body, it should open your mind to messages from the universe.

Check **Appendix II**: I have included 15 recipes from the drinks chapter of my book *The Kitchen Witch,* so you can try to prepare magical beverages!

## *Lucky Hands Wash*

This is a simple wash for your hands to attract luck your way.

You need:
- Nutmeg (1 teaspoon)
- Orange peels
- Boiling water
- Some moss

Get a metal bowl large enough to fit both your hands in. Pour the boiling water into the bowl until it is near the top. Sprinkle the nutmeg into the water and put it in the orange peels. Let it sit for a moment while the water cools and dip the moss into the water. Use the moss to wipe the water onto your hands or just soak your hands in the bowl.

# APPENDIX I
# HERBS LISTED BY ATTRIBUTES

### Herbs for
### Wealth, Abundance, Power, Success, and Prosperity:

Alfalfa, Almond, Alkanet, Ash, Acorn, Allspice, Basil, Benzoin, Blue Flag, Blackberry, Banana, Bladderwrack, Buckwheat, Bromeliad, Carnation, Camellia, Cashew, Chamomile, Club Moss, Comfrey, Cedar, Clove, Cinnamon, Cowslip, Calamus, Clover, Devil's Shoestring, Dill, Dock, Elder, Ebony, Fern, Fenugreek, Fumitory, Flax, Ginger, Gentian, Galangal, GoldenSeal, Grape, Gorse, Grains of Paradise, Honeysuckle, Heliotrope, Horse Chestnut, Honesty, High John the Conqueror, Irish Moss, Jasmine, Lemon Balm, Lucky Hand, Maple, Mint, Mandrake, Marjoram, May Apple, Moonwort, Myrtle, Moss, Nuts, Nutmeg, Onion, Oregon Grape, Oak, Orange, Oats, Pine, Pecan, Pineapple, Poppy, Periwinkle, Patchouli, Poplar, Pea, Pipsissewa, Pomegranate, Rowan, Rice, Rattlesnake Root, Sesame, Squill, Snapdragon, Sassafras, Snakeroot, Tulip, Tea, Tomato, Tonka, Trillium, Vetivert, Vervain, Wahoo, Woodruff, Winter's Bark, Wheat.

### Herbs for
### Attracting Love and Love Divination:

Adam and Eve, Acorn, Apple, Aster, Avocado, Aloe, Apricot, Avens, Balm of Gilead, Bachelor's Buttons, Basil, Bleeding Heart, Barley, Bloodroot, Bedstraw, Beans, Brazil Nut, Betony, Beet, Cheery, Chili Pepper, Caper, Chamomile, Catnip, Coriander, Crocus, Clover, Copal, Chickweed, Cardamom, Chestnut, Clove, Cinnamon, Clover, Columbine, Coltsfoot, Cuckoo-Flower, Cubeb,

Dodder, Daisy, Dill, Daffodil, Devil's Bit, Damiana, Dragon's Blood, Dogbane, Dutchman's Breeches, Elm, Elecampane, Eryngo, Endive, Fuzzy Weed, Fig, Ginger, Gentian, Grains of Paradise, Gardenia, Ginseng, Geranium, Hyacinth, Hibiscus, Hemp, Houseleek, High John the Conqueror, Jasmine, Juniper, Joe-Pye Weed, Kava-Kava, Lavender, Lettuce, Lime, Lemon Balm, Leek, Lemon Verbena, Lemon, Linden, Lotus, Lady's Mantle, Love Seed, Liverwort, Licorice, Lovage, Lovelia, Male Fern, Mullein, Mimosa, Mastic, Mandrake, Mallow, Marjoram, Myrtle, Mistletoe, Meadow Run, Moonwort, Maidenhair, Nuts, Orange, Oleander, Orchid, Papaya, Peach, Peppermint, Pansy, Poppy, Pea, Periwinkle, Plum, Prickly Ash, Primrose, Plumeria, Pimento, Purslane, Pear, Quince, Quassia, Rose, Rue, Rye, Raspberry, Rosemary, St. John's Wort, Skullcap, Strawberry, Spearmint, Sumbul, Sugar Cane, Senna, Saffron, Sarsaparilla, Spiderwort, Snakeroot, Southernwood, Sumbul, Thyme, Tonka, Tamarind, Tulip, Trillium, Tormentil, Tomato, Venus Flytrap, Valerian, Vanilla, Violet, Vervain, Vetivert, Wormwood, Willow, WitchGrass, Yohimbe, Yarrow, Yerba Mate.

### **Herbs for Lust:**

Avocado, Balsam, Carrot, Caper, Cat Tail, Caraway, Cinnamon, Celery, Dill, Daisy, Deer's Tongue, Damiana, Dulse, Eryngo, Endive, Garlic, Grains of Paradise, Galangal, Ginseng, Hibiscus, Licorice, Lemongrass, Mint, Maguey, Nettle, Onion, Olive, Patchouli, Parsley, Rosemary, Radish, Sesame, Southernwood, Saffron, Snakeroot, Violet, Vanilla, WitchGrass, Yohimbe, Yerba Mate.

### **Herbs for Reversing Love and Lust Magic:**

Camphor, Lettuce, Lotus, Lily, Pistachio, Vervain, and Witch Hazel.

## Herbs for
## Happiness, Peace, Tranquility, Harmony, and Sleep:

Agrimony, Cinquefoil, Chamomile, Catnip, Cyclamen, Celandine, Dulse, Datura, Eryngo, Elder, Gardenia, Hops, Hawthorn, Hyacinth, High John the Conqueror, Lavender, Linden, Lettuce, Loosestrife, Lily of the Valley, Morning Glory, Marjoram, Meadowsweet, Myrtle, Olive, Peppermint, Passion Flower, Purslane, Pennyroyal, Quince, Rosemary, Saffron, St. John's Wort, Skullcap, Thyme, Violet, Vervain, Valerian, WitchGrass.

## Herbs
## for Healing Spells and Health Blessings:

Ash, Allspice, Angelica, Anemone, Adder's Tongue, Amaranth, Apple, Bay, Balm of Gilead, Barley, Balsam, Burdock, Blackberry, Bracken, Bittersweet, Carnation, Calamus, Cinnamon, Cowslip, Coriander, Cedar, Citron, Caraway, Cucumber, Dock, Eucalyptus, Elder, Fennel, Fern, Flax, Figwort, Garlic, Galangal, Groundsel, Ginseng, GoldenSeal, Geranium, Gardenia, Goat's Rue, Henna, Hemp, Horehound, Heliotrope, Hops, Horse Chestnut, Ivy, Juniper, Job's Tears, Knotweed, Life-Everlasting, Larkspur, Lemon Balm, Lime, Mint, Mandrake, Mistletoe, Mugwort, Myrrh, Mesquite, Mullein Nutmeg, Marjoram, Nettle, Olive, Oak, Onion, Pepper Tree, Pimpernel, Pine, Plum, Peppermint, Persimmon, Plantain, Potato, Rue, Rose, Rowan, Rosemary, Sandalwood, Saffron, Spearmint, Sorrel, St. John's Wort, Sumbul, Sassafras, Spikenwood, Thyme, Thistle, Tansy, Ti, Violet, Vervain, Wintergreen, Willow, Walnut, Yerba Santa.

## Herbs for
## Protection and Strength:

African Violet, Ague Root, Acacia, Alyssum, Aloe, Althea, Anemone, Anise, Ash, Angelica, Amaranth, Agrimony, Asafoetida, Arbutus, Bay, Bamboo, Barley, Birch, Balm of Gilead, Blackberry, Boneset, Broom, Briony, Burdock, Buckthorn, Bittersweet, Basil, Bean,

Bloodroot, Bodhi, Betony, Blueberry, Bladderwrack, Bromeliad, Carnation, Cedar, Cactus, Calamus, Castor, Cinnamon, Caraway, Club Moss, Cotton, Clove, Curry, Cypress, Cumin, Celandine, Cinchona, Cascara Sagrada, Cinquefoil, Clover, Coconut, Cyclamen, Dill, Dragon's Blood, Datura, Dogwood, Devil's Bit, Devil's Shoestring, Elder, Eucalyptus, Ebony, Elecampane, Euphorbia, Figwort, Fern, Fennel, Foxglove, Flax, Feverwort, Frankincense, Fleabane, Garlic, Gorse, Grass, Grain, Ginseng, Galangal, Geranium, Gourd, Holly, Hazel, Houseleek, Honeysuckle, Heather, Hyssop, Hyacinth, Horehound, Ivy, Irish Moss, Juniper, Kava-Kava, Lavender, Lime, Leek, Larch, Lady's Slipper, Linden, Lotus, Larkspur, Lilac, Lucky Hand, Lily, Liquidambar, Loosestrife, Mugwort, Mallow, Meadow Rue, Mint, Marigold, Molluka, Mullein, Myrrh, Mustard, Masterwort, Mulberry, Mimosa, Mistletoe, Norfolk Pine, Nettle, Olive, Onion, Oak, Orris, Pennyroyal, Pilot Weed, Periwinkle, Pine, Plum, Pepper, Parsley, Pimpernel, Papyrus, Plantain, Papaya, Primrose, Purslane, Pepper Tree, Quince, Ragwort, Rice, Radish, Raspberry, Rose, Rattlesnake Root, Roots, Rhubarb, Rowan, Rosemary, Sandalwood, Sage, Snapdragon, Spanish Moss, St. John's Wort, Squill, Southernwood, Sloe, Saffron, Sweetpea, Tomato, Thistle, Tulip, Ti, Turnip, Tormentil, Tamarisk, Toadflax, Tea, Violet, Venus Flytrap, Vervain, Valerian, Willow, Wax Plant, Wolf's Bane, Wormwood, Witch Hazel, Woodruff, Wintergreen, Yucca, Yerba Santa.

### **Herbs for Wishes:**

Bay Leaf, Buckthorn, Bamboo, Beech, Dogwood, Dandelion, Grains of Paradise, Ginseng, Hazel, Job's Tears, Liquidambar, Pomegranate, Sunflower, Sage, Sandalwood, Tonka, Violet, Walnut.

### **Herbs for Beauty:**

Avocado, Chamomile, Flax, Ginseng, Lavender, Rose.

## Herbs for
### Friendship and Companionship:
Cinnamon, Love Seed, Lemon, Passion Flower, Rosemary, Sweet Pea,

## Herbs for
### Astral Projection, Dreams, and Divination:
Broom, Buchu, Bracken, Cinquefoil, Cherry, Camphor, Dandelion, Dittany of Crete, Fig, Ground Ivy, Goldenrod, Hibiscus, Heliotrope, Jasmine, Meadowsweet, Mugwort, Marigold, Mimosa, Orris, Orange, Onion, Pomegranate, Rose.

## Herbs for Luck:
Aloe, Acorn, Allspice, Be-Still, Bamboo, Banyan, Bluebell, ChinaBerry, Cotton, Cabbage, Cinchona, Calamus, Devil's Bit, Daffodil, Fern, Grains of Paradise, Holly, Hazel, Huckleberry, Heather, Houseleek, Irish Moss, Job's Tears, Lucky Hand, Linden, Moss, Male Fern, Nutmeg, Orange, Oak, Persimmon, Poppy, Pomegranate, Purslane, Pineapple, Rose, Straw, Snakeroot, Sumbul, Strawberry, Star Anise, Violet, Vetivert, Wood Rose.

## Herbs for
### Purification and Cleansing:
Anise, Avens, Alkanet, Arabic Gum, Asafoetida, Balsam, Bay, Betony, Benzoin, Broom, Bloodroot, Chamomile, Copal, Cedar, Coconut, Euphorbia, Fennel, Hyssop, Horseradish, Iris, Lemon, Lavender, Lemon Verbena, Mimosa, Marjoram, Pepper Tree, Parsley, Peppermint, Rosemary, Shallot, Sagebrush, Thyme, Turmeric, Thistle, Vervain, Valerian, Yucca.

# APPENDIX II
# RECIPES
## FROM THE BOOK *THE KITCHEN WITCH*.

## *Prophetic Dream Tea*
| Total time: 10 minutes; Servings: 6 |

Ingredients
- Chamomile – 1 teaspoon
- Rose petals – 2 teaspoons
- Cinnamon – 1/2 teaspoon
- Peppermint – 1 teaspoon
- Mugwort – 1 teaspoon

Instructions
1. Place all the ingredients in a small bowl, stir until mixed and store in a glass jar closed with a lid tightly.
2. When ready to cook tea, heat 1 cup of water until boiled, then pour into the cup, add 1 teaspoon of prepared tea mixture and let steep.
3. Then stir in sweetener to taste and serve.

## *After Dinner Carminative Tea*
| Total time: 40 minutes; Servings: 4 |

Ingredients
- Fennel seeds – 1 tablespoon
- Water – 1 cup

Instructions
1. Place a small saucepan over medium heat, pour in water, add fennel seeds and bring to boil.
2. Then remove the pan from the heat and let it for 15 minutes.
3. Pour the tea into a cup and serve.

## *Strawberry-Mint Sun Tea*

| Total time: 40 minutes; Servings: 8 |

Ingredients
- Sprigs of mint with leaves – 4
- Frozen whole strawberries – 30
- Honey – 8 teaspoon
- Ceylon tea – 4
- Cold water – 8 cups
- Ice cubes – as needed
- Strawberries, fresh – as needed for garnish
- Mint leaves, fresh – as needed for garnish

Instructions
1. Pour cold water in a large pitcher, add mint sprigs and Ceylon tea bag, then place the pitcher in direct sunlight, cover it and let the tea brew for 4 to 5 hours.
2. If you want to brew tea quickly, place a pot over medium heat, pour in 2 cups water, add mint sprigs and Ceylon tea, bring to boil and let the tea steep for 2 minutes.
3. Then remove and discard the tea bags, add half of the frozen strawberries, let sit for 10 minutes and stir.
4. Meanwhile, divide the remaining frozen strawberries and ice cubes evenly between six ice tea glasses and then top with mint leaves.
5. Discard mint sprigs from the tea, add honey, stir

well and then pour tea into ice tea glasses.
6. Serve straight away.

## *Self-Love Coffee*
| Total time: 10 minutes; Servings: 1 |

Ingredients
- Coffee grounds 2 tablespoons
- Whole cloves – 2
- Allspice – ½ teaspoon
- Ground cinnamon – ½ teaspoon
- Sugar – 1 teaspoon
- Milk or cream – As needed

Instructions
1. Place coffee grounds in a bowl, add cloves and stir well.
2. Then stir in allspice and cinnamon until well mixed and spoon the mixture into a coffee filter and prepare the coffee as required.
3. Then add sugar, stir well until completely dissolve, then add milk or cream and serve.

## *Magical Coffee*
| Total time: 10 minutes; Servings: 1 |

Ingredients
- Ground ginger – 3 pinches
- Ground cinnamon – 3 pinches
- Ground nutmeg – 1/8 teaspoon
- Ground coffee – 1 tablespoon

Instructions
1. Place ground coffee and cinnamon in a mug and stir until mixed.
2. Add nutmeg and ginger and stir until blend.

3. Then process the coffee in the coffee filter as required and serve.

## *Ostara Lavender Lemonade*

|Total time: 10 minutes; Servings: 8 |

Ingredients
- Lavender, dried – 2 tablespoons
- Sugar – 1 ½ cup
- Honey – 1 ½ tablespoon
- Lemon juice – 1 ½ cup
- Water – 8 cups

Instructions
1. Place a pot over medium-high heat, pour in 1 cup water, add sugar, stir well and bring to boil until sugar is dissolved completely.
2. Then add honey and lavender, stir well until incorporated and remove the pot from heat.
3. Cool the lemonade, then pour into a pitcher, pour in the remaining water, add lemon juice and mix well.
4. Chill lemonade in the refrigerator and then serve.

## *Ginger Mojito*

|Total time: 5 minutes; Servings: 1 |

Ingredients
- Lime, cut into 8 wedges – 1
- Mint Leaves, fresh – as needed
- Honey – 2 tablespoons
- Ginger Beer – 12-ounce
- Rum – 3-ounce
- Ice cubes – 6

Instructions

1. Place lime wedges in a cocktail mixer, add mint, then pour in rum and muddle well.
2. Take a large cocktail glass, add ice and honey and mint leaves and then evenly pour in rum mixture.
3. Serve mojito with lime.

## *Black Apple Mojito*

|Total time: 5 minutes; Servings: 1 |

Ingredients
- Blackberries, fresh – 5
- Blueberries, fresh – 6
- Fresh mint leaves – 15
- Lime juice – 2 tablespoons
- Apple cider – 6 ounce
- Light rum – 2 ounce
- Ice cubes – 4

Instructions
1. Pour rum in a cocktail mixer, add berries and mint leaves and muddle all the ingredients until berries and mint leaves are crushed and release their juices.
2. Add ice, pour in apple juice and lime juice and shake well until combined.
3. Strain out ice cubes from the mojito, pour the drink in a large cocktail glass and serve with blueberries.

## *Natural Energy Drink*

|Total time: 5 minutes; Servings: 1 |

Ingredients
- Apple slices – 3

- Sugar – 1 teaspoon
- Lemon juice – 1 tablespoon
- Orange juice – 1 ½ tablespoon
- Frozen lemonade, thawed – as needed

Instructions
1. Place all the ingredients except for lemonade in a bottle, then fill with thawed lemonade and close the bottle.
2. Shake the bottle well for 1 minute or until ingredients are well combined and then chill the drink for 4 hours or overnight.
3. Serve straight away.

## *Mabon Cider*

|Total time: 35 minutes; Servings: 4 |

Ingredients
- Whole cloves – 1 teaspoon
- Salt – 1/3 teaspoon
- Brown sugar – 1/3 cup
- Ground nutmeg – 1/8 teaspoon
- Apple cider – 2 quarts

Instructions
1. Place a saucepan over medium heat, add all the ingredients for cider, stir well and bring the mixture to boil.
2. Then lower the heat to medium level and simmer for 30 minutes.
3. Strain the cider into a pitcher, serve straight away or chill before serving.

## *Hot Berry Cider*

|Total time: 35 minutes; Servings: 10 |

Ingredients
- Allspice berries – 4
- Whole cloves – 4
- Cinnamon sticks, halves – 1
- Apple cider – 8 cups
- Cranberry juice cocktail – 16 ounce

Instructions
1. Place a saucepan over medium heat, add all the ingredients for cider, stir well and bring the mixture to boil.
2. Then lower the heat to medium level and simmer for 30 minutes.
3. Strain the cider into a pitcher, serve straight away or chill before serving.

## *Rosemary Tonic Wine*

| Total time: 40 minutes; Servings: 4 |

Ingredients
- sprigs of rosemary, fresh – 6
- Bottle of white wine – 1

Instructions
1. Pour out a little wine from its bottle, then insert rosemary sprigs until immersed completely into wine and close the bottle with its cork.
2. Place the bottle in a cool and dark place and let rest for 2 weeks.
3. Then strain the herbs from the wine, pour the wine in tonic glasses and serve.

## *Cinnamon Tonic Wine*

| Total time: 5 minutes; Servings: 4 |

Ingredients
- Bottle of red wine – 1
- Cinnamon stick – 1

Instructions
1. Pour out a little wine from its bottle, then insert cinnamon stick until immersed completely into wine and close the bottle with its cork.
2. Place the bottle in a cool and dark place and let rest for 1 week.
3. Remove and discard cinnamon stick from the wine, pour the wine in tonic glasses, and serve.

## *Mulled Wine*

| Total time: 10 minutes; Servings: 4 |

Ingredients
- Hibiscus tea – 2 cups
- Water – 2 cups
- Orange, sliced – 1
- Honey – 5 teaspoons

Spices:
1. Cinnamon stick – 1
2. Whole cloves – 8
3. Anise star – 2
4. Vanilla pods – ½ teaspoon

Instructions
1. Place a pot over medium heat, add water and tea, and bring to boil.
2. Then place another pot over medium heat, add all the spices, pour in ½ cup water, bring to boil and let cook for 1 minute.
3. Add orange slices, pour in tea, honey and stir well until honey dissolves.

4. Serve immediately.

## Herbal Liqueur

| Total time: 10 minutes; Servings: 2 |

Ingredients
- Mint leaves, chopped – 2 cups
- Honey – ¾ cup
- Vodka – 1 ½ cups
- Water – 3/4 cup

Instructions
1. Place mint leaves in a glass pitcher, pour in vodka, let cover tightly with its lid, then place the pitcher in a cool and dark place and let stand for 6 weeks, shaking every few days.
2. Then place a pot over medium heat, add honey, pour in water, stir well and cook for 5 minutes or more until honey dissolve and when done, let the mixture cool.
3. Strain vodka mixture through a strainer, add honey mixture and stir well.
4. Serve straight away.

If you liked this book, let me know with a comment on Amazon. It is very important for me to know your opinion. Thank you.

# BIBLIOGRAPHY

- Astrological Correspondences. (2019). Sacredwicca.com. Retrieved 23 July 2019, from https://sacredwicca.com/astrological-correspondences
- A Wiccan Guide to Moon Magic – Wicca Living. (2019). Wicca Living. Retrieved 23 July 2019, from http://wiccaliving.com/wiccan-full-moon-ritual/
- A Brief Summary of Core Wiccan Beliefs. (2019). Wicca Living. Retrieved 23 July 2019, from http://wiccaliving.com/essentials-wicca/
- Popular Wiccan Traditions: Different Forms of Wicca. (2019). Wicca Living. Retrieved 23 July 2019, from http://wiccaliving.com/wiccan-traditions-wicca-forms/
- Beginners Guide to Herbal Magic for Wiccans – Wicca Living. (2019). Wicca Living. Retrieved 23 July 2019, from http://wiccaliving.com/beginners-guide-herbal-magic/
- Elemental Magic for Beginners: Basic Principles - Craft of Wicca. (2019). Craft of Wicca. Retrieved 24 July 2019, from https://craftofwicca.com/elemental-magic-for-beginners/
- Creating an elemental garden. (2019). Gardensforeverybody.blogspot.com. Retrieved 24 July 2019, from http://gardensforeverybody.blogspot.com/2012/08/creating-elemental-garden.html
- 14 Magical Tools for Pagan Practice. (2019). Learn Religions. Retrieved 31 July 2019, from https://www.learnreligions.com/magical-tools-for-pagan-practice-4064607
- Composting Leaves: How to Make Organic Plant Food - Home for the Harvest. (2016). Home for the Harvest. Retrieved 31 July 2019, from https://www.homefortheharvest.com/composting-leaves/

- How to Create a Witch's Garden. (2019). Exemplore. Retrieved 31 July 2019, from https://exemplore.com/wicca-witchcraft/How-to-Create-a-Witchs-Garden
- How to Harvest, Dry, and Store Your Magical Herbs. (2019). Learn Religions. Retrieved 1 August 2019, from https://www.learnreligions.com/harvesting-drying-and-storing-magical-herbs-2562025
- Herbs Correspondences. (2019). Sacredwicca.com. Retrieved 2 August 2019, from https://sacredwicca.com/herbs-correspondences
- A Witch's glossary of herbs. (2017). Grove and Grotto. Retrieved 2 August 2019, from https://www.groveandgrotto.com/blogs/articles/a-witchs-glossary-of-herbs
- Herb Correspondences: Magic Herbs - Herb Magick. (2019). Spelwerx.com. Retrieved 2 August 2019, from https://www.spelwerx.com/herb_correspondences.html
- A Beginners Guide to Magical Oils: Essential Oils Magic. (2019). Wicca Living. Retrieved 3 August 2019, from http://wiccaliving.com/beginners-guide-magical-oils/
- ESSENTIAL OIL TIPS . (2019). Joellessacredgrove.com. Retrieved 3 August 2019, from http://www.joellessacredgrove.com/Herbs/eoils.html
- Watch Out for These Dangerous Herbs!. (2019). Learn Religions. Retrieved 4 August 2019, from https://www.learnreligions.com/toxic-and-poisonous-herbs-256

CPSIA information can be obtained
at www.ICGtesting.com
Printed in the USA
LVHW051731240920
667015LV00004B/798